The Making of a Martyr

An Analysis of the Indictments of Donald Trump

John H. Wilson

ISBN: 9798878550123

ACKNOWLEDGMENTS

This book would not be possible without the support of several people.

My First - I wish to thank Frank Vernuccio and the Staff at the Vernuccio/Novak Report and usagovpolicy.com for their friendship, support, encouragement, and most of all, for giving me a place to express my thoughts, opinions, analysis, outrage, sarcasm, and dark humor on the ongoing prosecution of former President Donald Trump, as well as other topics. Freedom of Expression and the First Amendment are alive and well at these outlets, and in the hearts of Frank and his team. Many of the following chapters have appeared in whole or in part at usagovpolicy.com over the years.

My Last - I wish to thank my former law school classmate and Court Attorney, Alan Flexer, Esq. An unwavering voice of reason, sanity and common sense, Alan has served as my consigliere for many years, both in "peace" and "wartime." Many of our discussions would begin with "did you mean to say it this way?" As usual, Alan, you are right. Your advice and friendship are invaluable to me, and always will be.

My Everything - I wish to thank my partner in love, Susan Singer. A beautiful mind in a beautiful woman, her keen intellect has served as an inspiration to me, even when we were no more than two friends talking over coffee after Sunday Mass while our children ran around making nuisances of themselves. Thank you always for your love and support, and for listening to (and sharing your own opinions of) my views and thoughts.

A Special Acknowledgment must also be added for my son, John. Without him, all my efforts are for nothing. I thank God every day for making me your father.

TABLE OF CONTENTS

INTRODUCTION
THE SWAMP FIGHTS BACK

There is no denying it - Donald John Trump, the 45th President of the United States, is a polarizing figure. From June 16, 2015, the day he descended to the lobby of Trump Tower in New York City and announced his candidacy for the Office of the President, to the present day, Trump seems to inspire only two emotions, both in the extreme - love and hate.

Writing in *Town and Country Magazine,* Nell Scovell states that "Trump has taught me to hate things that never seemed worthy of hatred, items like: The number '45'...most presidents aren't recognized by their sequential number...Trump has embraced '45,' putting it on his golf hat and embroidering it on his cuffs. Many elevators skip the '13th floor' because it's considered bad luck. In the future, we will skip from 44 to 46...[t]he color orange. Orange still doesn't rhyme with any words, but it's now synonymous with Trump whose nicknames include Agent Orange, the Mango Mussolini, the Cheeto in Charge, and Tangerine Jesus. Orange is now off-color forever...[w]ords like 'sir,' 'hoax,' 'sad,' and 'huge.' How one man could ruin so many monosyllabic words is both sad and huge." [1]

Some of the hatred expressed for the "Bad Orange Man" isn't so tongue in cheek. One writer to *The Citizen Times* asked for help in controlling his "Trump derangement syndrome"; "My problem is that I hate - I have a complete, visceral, and uncompromising

---

[1] Nell Scovell, Town & Country, "One Writer's End of Term List: 10 Things I Now Hate Because of Trump", November 17, 2020

repulsion towards - anyone who supports Donald Trump... All I have to do is open the newspaper, read of Trump's latest atrocity, and I'm again filled with hatred. Hatred for the man himself...And, maybe most of all, hatred for the 40 percent of American voters who seem incapable of understanding that if Trump succeeds in destroying the Constitution on his mad drive to become America's first dictator, he'll take down THEM, too." [2]

Tom Treece, writing in the *Monroe News*, makes this observation; "[L]et me agree with Trump-haters that Donald Trump is a narcissistic, egotistical bully and despite my support for his policies, I'm almost glad he's out of our everyday life... I remember being outraged the evening Michigan Rep. Rashida Talib was sworn in to Congress (and before Donald Trump ever served a day in the White House). In her comments she recanted telling her son, 'We're gonna impeach the mother---ker.' And liberals were upset with Trump's verbiage? Then the mainstream media - specifically CBS, NBC, ABC, MSNBC and CNN - methodically trashed Trump EVERY day for the next four years. No matter what he did, they criticized him daily." [3]

The *HF Tornado*, the student newspaper of Harborfields High School in Greenlawn, New York, offers an explanation for this pathological Trump-hatred, an explanation that should have occurred to more experienced journalists; "Donald Trump is not a politician. He is a businessman...[h]e took a 'no filter' mentality with him while debating, giving speeches, and speaking publicly. This...made people hate him. Some of the things he said were unlike any other president in history...[m]ost importantly, a huge mass of the public was led to hate Donald Trump for one single reason. His presence in the White House exposed lying, corruption, and bad character inside the United States government. No other president in history has done this. His attitude as a businessman let him, without trying sometimes, expose the true nature of how portions of our government function."[4]

---

[2] Anonymous, Citizen-Times, "Ask John: How do I get rid of my hatred for Trump and his supporters?", March 12, 2019

[3] Tom Treece, The Monroe News, "Biden is president because of hatred for Trump", December 27, 2021

[4] Anonymous, HF Tornado, "Editorial: What Makes Donald Trump The Most

The HF Tornado Editorial goes on to point out that "[t]he media, which is often aligned with the Democratic party, has now come up with a highly sophisticated system to censor this information being exposed. Since Donald Trump is exposing details about government officials that the Democratic party and the big tech companies didn't want you to see, they hid it so you couldn't see it. Instead, they made him out to be the most racist person ever, who was only in the White House to promote white supremacy."

Both the young writers at *The HF Tornado* and Treece recognize one common factor in the stoking of hatred of the 45th President - the constant drumbeat of the media, fanning the fires of that hatred on a daily basis. But the media is only a tool, used by the people who really have it out for Trump - the Professional Political Establishment of Washington DC; that is "The Swamp."

It is no secret that there is a group of people who are entrenched in the corridors of power. This is human nature; from the bureaucrats of Ancient Egypt who served the Pharaohs, to the Ministers who provided advise to the Kings and Queens of Medieval Europe, there have always been people who attach themselves to power and try to take control of their leaders and their society by manipulating the appointed or elected head of that society.

Conversely, those in power make use of these sycophants to maintain and expand their hold on leadership and the resultant power. It is a symbiotic relationship, almost primitive in nature, which has withstood centuries of the rise and fall of various human institutions.

In Washington DC, the professional bureaucrats of the recent past prided themselves on being "above" politics and being able to serve any elected administration regardless of their own party affiliation, or that of the President. Similarly, the press also took a more neutral stance towards those in power or authority, at least in the years following the Andrew Jackson presidency. "All the News that's fit to print" used to be read as a commitment to give the reader the information needed to make their own decision.

Now that motto should read, "All the News we believe to be fit for you to agree with our overtly progressive position."

Presidents have always nominated their supporters to their Cabinets, and to leadership positions in various federal agencies. But

---

Hated President In United States History?", November 9, 2020

beginning in the Clinton years, and continuing with a vengeance under the Obama presidency, the professional bureaucrats who worked for the Partisan Appointees have been replaced with people who were more loyal to both of these Administrations and to the Democratic Party than to the Institution which employed them. Messianic in their outlook, these acolytes of progressive political structures followed the path laid down by Barak Obama in a rare moment of utter honesty expressed on October 30, 2008, just prior to his election; "We are five days away from fundamentally transforming the United States of America." [5]

This "fundamental transformation" was supposed to continue in one form or another with the election of Hillary Clinton in 2016. But instead, the unthinkable happened - the anti-politician businessman, Donald J. Trump, was elected President of the United States.

The 45th President did much to halt the rise of progressive control of Washington, DC, and in turn, the rest of the nation. But not enough. His Administration found itself hampered from within, as in particular, lawyers in both the Justice Department and FBI who were holdovers from prior administrations, "worked together to thwart President Trump's presidency just as it got underway." As described in *Investor's Business Daily*, "Congress released documents (in September of 2018) showing an 'apparent systemic culture of media leaking" among top officials at the FBI and Justice Department...[i]n particular...text messages exchanged on April 10 and April 12, 2017, between former FBI agent Peter Strzok and his then-lover, former FBI attorney Lisa Page, explicitly discuss the FBI's 'media leak strategy.'"

But this was only the tip of the Iceberg. "As Fox News reports, "The leaks involved other outlets in addition to *The Washington Post*. ... FBI and DOJ officials, including DOJ prosecutor and top Robert Mueller deputy Andrew Weissman, met with several Associated Press reporters in April 2017." According to then-North Carolina Republican Rep. Mark Meadows, "[t]he leaks to the media continued even as FBI attorneys cited the U.S. Attorney's Manual in telling Congress that witnesses could not answer questions about pending probes."[6]

---

[5] Paul Kengor, National Catholic Register, "How Barack Obama Fundamentally Transformed the United States", January 12, 2017

[6] Editorial, Investor's Business Daily, "FBI's 'leak strategy': Was it criminal

For the first two years of the Trump Presidency, this "media leak strategy" involved claims of "Russian Interference" in the 2016 Presidential Election, and allegations that the Trump campaign had been "in collusion" with the Russian government. Many of these allegations came from a "dossier" prepared by Christopher Steele, a former member of British Intelligence, which "contained numerous allegations about connections between Trump's 2016 presidential campaign and the Kremlin, and also included allegations of salacious sexual activity that Trump supposedly engaged in at a Moscow hotel." [7]

As described by *The Associated Press*, however, it turns out that the source of Steele's information, Igor Danchenko, "told an FBI agent he was shocked and dismayed that the speculative information he provided was portrayed as fact."[8]

In other words, the basis for the "Russian collusion" allegation was a lie. However, this allegation was taken seriously enough that in May of 2017, "Deputy Attorney General Rod Rosenstein...appointed former FBI Director Robert Mueller to serve as special counsel to oversee the previously confirmed FBI investigation of Russian efforts to influence the 2016 presidential election and related matters."[9]

In March of 2019, after months of investigations, what were the major findings of the Report published by Special Counsel Mueller? "The investigation did not establish that members of the Trump campaign conspired or coordinated with the Russian government in its election interference activities."[10]

And just how did this "Steele dossier" come to be created? "Hillary Clinton's 2016 presidential campaign...hired [the law firm of] Perkins Coie, which then hired Fusion GPS, a research and intelligence firm, to conduct opposition research on Republican candidate Donald Trump's ties to Russia...research that eventually became the infamous Steele dossier."[11] In fact, both the Clinton

---

collusion to damage Trump?", September 11, 2018.

[7] Matthew Barakat, AP News, "Trump dossier source shocked speculation portrayed as fact", October 13, 2022

[8] Ibid.

[9] Paula Reid, CBS News, "Robert Mueller appointed special counsel", May 17, 2017

[10] Robert S. Mueller, III, "Report on the Investigation into Russian Interference in the 2016 Presidential Election", Volume I of II, March 2019

[11] Jill Colvin, AP News, "DNC, Clinton campaign agree to Steele dossier funding fine", March 31, 2022

Campaign and the Democratic National Committee "agreed to pay $113,000 to settle a Federal Election Commission investigation into whether they violated campaign finance law. "'By intentionally obscuring their payments through Perkins Coie and failing to publicly disclose the true purpose of those payments,' the campaign and DNC 'were able to avoid publicly reporting on their statutorily required FEC disclosure forms the fact that they were paying Fusion GPS to perform opposition research on Trump with the intent of influencing the outcome of the 2016 presidential election,' the initial (FEC) complaint had read."[12]

An ironic development, given some of the charges brought against former President Trump, which will be discussed in more detail in the following pages.

More importantly, how did this Steele dossier become the basis for the Mueller investigation? As the sequence of events is described in *The Hill*, it was used by the FBI as the basis for a warrant used to conduct surveillance on the Trump campaign. Yet, the warrant application, issued under the Foreign Intelligence Surveillance Act (FISA), failed to mention "that the British intelligence operative's work was opposition research connected to Hillary Clinton's campaign and might be biased." [13]

Associate Attorney General Bruce Ohr, testified before Congress that he "briefed both senior FBI and DOJ officials in summer 2016 [and] explicitly warned them...Steele expressed bias against Trump and was working on a project connected to the Clinton campaign."[14]

Nonetheless, the warrant application submitted by the FBI to the FISA court "did not mention any connection to the DNC or Clinton. Rather, it referred to Steele as a reliable source in past criminal investigations who was hired by a person working for a U.S. law firm to conduct research on Trump and Russia." The FBI also stated that it was "'unaware of any derogatory information' about Steele, that Steele was 'never advised … as to the motivation behind the research' but that the FBI speculates' that those who hired Steele were 'likely looking for information to discredit' Trump's campaign."[15]

---

[12] Ibid.

[13] John Solomon, The Hill, "FISA shocker: DOJ official warned Steele dossier was connected to Clinton, might be biased", January 16, 2019

[14] Ibid.

[15] Ibid.

Significantly, "[s]ignatures from top FBI and Justice Department officials, including...Deputy Attorney General Rod Rosenstein appear on each of the [warrant] applications."[16] Remember Rosenstein? He's the one who appointed Robert Mueller to conduct an investigation on the allegations of "Russian collusion".

In other words, members of the FBI and Justice Department used false information that came from the Clinton Campaign to secure a warrant to conduct surveillance on the campaign of her opponent, Donald J. Trump. These same officials then leaked this information to the press, creating a public perception that Trump and his campaign were in collusion with a foreign power. Then, based upon the media outcry, these same officials appointed a Special Prosecutor to investigate these false allegations.

And after two years and millions of dollars spent, the investigation revealed that the allegations had been false all along.

Not satisfied with this extensive effort to damage Donald Trump at the dawn of his Administration, "The Swamp", that loose confederation of professional bureaucrats left over from the Obama Administration, and the Democratic officeholders they support, hit upon another method to keep the Trump Administration off-balance. Thus was born the First Impeachment of Donald J. Trump.

As described by Jacob G. Hornberger, the founder and president of The Future of Freedom Foundation writing for the Mises Institute, "hatred so consumed the Left and the mainstream press that they spent the first two years convincing themselves, falsely, that Trump was a covert Russian agent, one whose assignment was to deliver America into the clutches of the nation's Cold War rival. When that investigation went nowhere, it was followed by Impeachment I, which also went nowhere."[17]

The first effort to impeach President Trump began with a telephone call to the then newly-elected President of the Ukraine, Volodymyr Zelensky, on July 25, 2019, in which Trump stated "there's been a lot of talk about [Joe] Biden's son [Hunter Biden], that Biden stopped the prosecution and a lot of people want to find out about that…Biden went around bragging that he stopped the

---

[16] Jeremy Herb, and David Shortell, CNN, "FBI releases Carter Page surveillance warrant documents", July 23, 2018

[17] Jacob G. Hornberger, Jacob G., Mises Institute, "Why They Hate Trump So Deeply", January 19, 2021

prosecution so if you could look into it…It sounds horrible to me."[18]

In fact, former Vice President Joe Biden did "brag" that he had been instrumental in getting that same prosecutor removed from office, by threatening to withhold a billion dollars in funding from the Ukraine if this prosecutor was not fired.[19] Further, that same prosecutor had been involved in investigating a Ukrainian Natural Gas company that had hired Hunter Biden, who had no experience in the natural gas business, but is the son of the then Vice President of the United States, Joe Biden.

But regardless of these facts, The House of Representatives, with a Democratic majority led by then-Speaker Nancy Pelosi, voted to impeach President Trump. As described by the BBC, "In December [2019], Democratic leaders in the US House of Representatives unveiled two impeachment charges - abuse of power and the obstruction of Congress. Then, a week before Christmas, the House voted to impeach Mr Trump, ensuring that he became only the third US president to suffer the same fate (after Andrew Johnson and Bill Clinton). Over two weeks in January and February 2020, the Senate held a trial. A Senate vote requires a two-thirds majority to convict, so a guilty verdict was always unlikely given that Mr Trump's party controls the chamber. And this is how it came to pass. Mr Trump was cleared - by 52 votes to 48 on one count, and 53 votes to 47 on the other."[20]

Having failed twice to force the removal of Donald Trump from the office of the President, the 2020 Presidential Election succeeded where "The Swamp" and the Democratic Party had failed before - Barak Obama's Vice President, Joe Biden, was declared the winner.

Donald Trump did not take defeat lightly. "This is a fraud on the American public," Trump said on November 4, 2020, Election Night. "This is an embarrassment to our country. We were getting ready to win this election. Frankly, we did win this election. We did win this election. So our goal now is to ensure the integrity for the good of this nation. This is a very big moment. This is a major fraud

---

[18] Staff, Politico, "Read the Trump-Ukraine phone call readout", September 25, 2019

[19] dagalagas, YouTube, "Joe Biden Brags about getting Ukrainian Prosecutor Fired", updated September 8, 2023

[20] Anonymous, BBC, "Trump impeachment: The short, medium and long story", February 5, 2020

in our nation...It's a very sad moment. To me this is a very sad moment, and we will win this. And as far as I'm concerned, we already have won it."[21]

For months, the Trump Campaign made various efforts to overturn the results of the 2020 Presidential Election. Numerous lawsuits were brought in various states, including Arizona, Pennsylvania, Nevada, and Georgia. None were ultimately successful.

Then, in a last-ditch effort to forestall the inevitable, Trump asked Vice-President Mike Pence to stop the Certification of the vote of the Electoral College. "It is my considered judgment that my oath to support and defend the Constitution constrains me from claiming unilateral authority to determine which electoral votes should be counted and which should not," Pence wrote in a letter to Congress, dated January 6, 2020.[22]

As is well-known, on that same day, Donald Trump held a rally for his supporters in Washington DC at the Ellipse, a park located South of the White House fence and North of Constitution Avenue, less than 3 miles from the Capitol. "All of us here today do not want to see our election victory stolen by emboldened radical-left Democrats, which is what they're doing," Trump said. "And stolen by the fake news media. That's what they've done and what they're doing. We will never give up, we will never concede. It doesn't happen. You don't concede when there's theft involved." He also said "[o]ur country has had enough. We will not take it anymore and that's what this is all about. And to use a favorite term that all of you people really came up with: We will stop the steal. Today I will lay out just some of the evidence proving that we won this election and we won it by a landslide. This was not a close election."[23]

Near the conclusion of the speech, Trump said, "we will drain the Washington swamp and we will clean up the corruption in our nation's capital...So we're going to, we're going to walk down Pennsylvania Avenue. I love Pennsylvania Avenue. And we're going

---

[21] Donald Trump, @rev, "Donald Trump 2020 Election Night Speech Transcript", November 4, 2020

[22] Alana Wise, NPR, "Pence Says He Doesn't Have Power To Reject Electoral Votes", January 6, 2021

[23] Brian Naylor NPR, "Read Trump's Jan. 6 Speech, A Key Part Of Impeachment Trial", February 10, 2021

to the Capitol, and we're going to try and give...our Republicans, the weak ones because the strong ones don't need any of our help. We're going to try and give them the kind of pride and boldness that they need to take back our country. So, let's walk down Pennsylvania Avenue."[24]

But Trump never did take that walk down Pennsylvania Avenue. Instead, a large crowd, many already located outside the Capitol before and during the Trump rally at the Ellipse, began to enter the building, and travel through areas that were off limits, including the floor of the House and the offices of several Representatives. Much of the crowd was non-violent, wandering around like tourists; others clashed with police, damaged windows, and destroyed other property.

Depending on which side of the political aisle you sit, this event is either an "insurrection," or a "riot." Coverage at *CNN* includes headlines like "Jan 6 Insurrection at the US Capitol", "Timeline of the coup; how Trump tried to weaponize the Justice Department to overturn the 2020 election", and "Assault on Democracy: Paths to Insurrection".[25] Meanwhile, the *BBC* refers to the event as the "Capitol Riot",[26] as does *The History Channel*.[27]

Either way, Donald Trump was blamed for the violence, and even though he was only going to be in office for three more weeks, the House of Representatives moved quickly to bring a Second Article of Impeachment against the soon-to-be former President.

What could be the purpose of impeaching an out-going President? As Ed Kilgore of *New York Magazine* explained, "there is a case increasingly being made for proceeding with impeachment and forcing a Senate trial of Trump that would conclude *after* January 20 in order to ban him from holding office in the future."[28]

This theory is based on an interpretation of the 14th Amendment to the United States Constitution, which states "[n]o person shall be a Senator or Representative in Congress, or elector of President and Vice-President, or hold any office, civil or military, under the United

---

[24] Ibid.

[25] Anonymous, CNN, "January 6 insurrection at the US Capitol", undated

[26] Anonymous, BBC, "Capitol riots timeline: What happened on 6 January 2021?", August 2, 2023

[27] Editors, History.com, "This Day in History 2021 US Capitol riot", January 6, 2023

[28] Ed Kilgore, Intelligencer, "Impeachment Could Ban Trump From Running in 2024", January 8, 2021

States, or under any state, who, having previously taken an oath, as a member of Congress, or as an officer of the United States, or as a member of any State legislature, or as an executive or judicial officer of any State, to support the Constitution of the United States, shall have engaged in insurrection or rebellion against the same."[29]

Obviously then, the proponents of the Second Impeachment hoped to keep Donald Trump from running for office again by charging him with "Incitement of Insurrection".[30] However, these hopes were dashed when the Second Impeachment met the same fate as the first; "Donald Trump has been acquitted by the Senate...for his role in the 6 January attack on the US Capitol," according to *The Guardian*. "From the outset, Trump's allies in the Senate made clear they had no intention of convicting him...they relied on a technical argument, advanced by [Trump's] attorneys...that the proceedings were unconstitutional because Trump was no longer in office." [31]

For most former Presidents, this would be the end of the story. Most former Presidents settle into a routine of book writing, speech giving and the occasional diplomatic mission.

But Donald Trump is most certainly not like any prior former President.

Even before he officially announced his intention to run for re-election in 2024 in November of 2022, it was widely feared by "The Swamp" that Trump would run again. The trepidation of these professional bureaucrats and their Democratic Party masters is not unjustified. "[W]e will be taking on the most corrupt forces and entrenched interests imaginable," Trump stated in announcing his candidacy. "Our country is in a horrible state. We're in grave trouble...Our country is being destroyed before your very eyes...I am your voice. The Washington establishment wants to silence us, but we will not let them do that. What we have built together over the past six years is the greatest movement in history because it is not about politics. It's about our love for this great country, America."[32]

---

[29] Laura Temme, Findlaw, "Disqualification from Public Office Under the 14th Amendment", undated

[30] Brian Naylor NPR, "Article Of Impeachment Cites Trump's 'Incitement' Of Capitol Insurrection", February 9, 2021

[31] Sam Levine, and Lauren Gambino, The Guardian, "Donald Trump acquitted in second impeachment trial", February 13, 2021

Since leaving office in 2021, Donald John Trump has been subjected to an onslaught of lawsuits and criminal indictments. His home has been searched; His businesses have been subjected to legal proceedings. He has been harassed, prosecuted, and made the subject of an orchestrated campaign with one goal - to keep him out of the White House in 2024.

"Lawfare", it's been called, a play on the word "Warfare", but with the same violent intention as the waging of a war - Stopping Donald John Trump from resuming the Office of the President, by any means necessary.

In this book, we will examine the various criminal charges which have been brought against the 45th President. As a lawyer with over 30 years of experience as a prosecutor, defense attorney, and criminal court judge, I will use my legal expertise to review, examine and explain the criminal statutes Donald Trump is accused of violating, as well as the factual basis for these charges.

As you may be able to tell from this Introduction, it is my belief that the legal system is being used and abused by people who seek to "get" Trump. Their goal is simple and is stated up front by many - to keep the former President out of the Oral Office. Many consider their intentions to be noble, truly believing Trump to be an insurrectionist and a danger to our nation. Others are acting out of a white-hot hatred of the man. Still others wish only to maintain their power and authority.

Whatever the case, their efforts are misguided at best and illegal at worst. As we will see in the coming chapters, Donald John Trump is absolutely correct about one thing in particular:

This really is the greatest witch hunt in history.

---

[32] Donald Trump, @rev, "Former President Trump announces 2024 presidential bid Transcript", November 16, 2022

1 "NO REASONABLE PROSECUTOR WOULD BRING SUCH A CASE"

Before we consider the various criminal allegations brought against former President Trump, it would be helpful to review what could have been - the FBI investigation of Hillary Clinton prior to the 2016 Presidential election.

According to *The Washington Post*, "[t]he debate over what is to be done with Donald Trump and his alleged mishandling of sensitive government documents has landed in the zone where it was inevitably headed: whataboutism. Hillary Clinton escaped prosecution for using a private email server as secretary of state in 2016, the right argues, so why should Trump be indicted?"[33]

Indeed. Many people may remember that former Secretary of State Hillary Clinton was investigated for the mishandling of government documents, and at the time, there were calls for her prosecution. "Lock her up!" was the chant heard during the 2016 Republican convention.[34]

Yet, Clinton was not prosecuted, leading many to ask now what the difference is between the "crimes" both she and Donald Trump are alleged to have committed.

To answer, let us take a brief trip down the memory hole.

"Clinton's email troubles started in 2014, when the House Select Committee on Benghazi asked the State Department for all of her

---

[33] Aaron Blake, The Washington Post, "What about Clinton's emails? How Trump's document controversy differs", August 30, 2022

[34] Nick Gass, Politico, "'Lock her up' chant rules Republican convention", July 20, 2016

emails. The department didn't have them all because, instead of only using the State Department email system...Clinton used a personal email address...housed on private servers located in her Chappaqua, New York, home. In 2014, Clinton's lawyers combed through the private server and turned over about 30,000 work-related emails to the State Department and deleted the rest, which Clinton said involved personal matters, such as her daughter's wedding plans. Clinton repeatedly said she did not have any classified emails on her server..."[35]

On July 5, 2016, then-FBI Director James Comey held a press conference, and gave a detailed statement regarding a criminal investigation his department had conducted regarding Clinton's "use of a personal e-mail system during her time as Secretary of State." In particular, the investigation "focused on whether classified information was transmitted on that personal system."[36]

"Secretary Clinton used several different servers and administrators of those servers during her four years at the State Department," then-Director Comey explained, "and used numerous mobile devices to view and send e-mail on that personal domain." Further, "FBI investigators...also read all of the approximately 30,000 e-mails provided by Secretary Clinton to the State Department in December 2014... [f]rom [this] group of 30,000 e-mails...110 e-mails in 52 e-mail chains have been determined...to contain classified information at the time they were sent or received. Eight of those chains contained information that was Top Secret at the time they were sent; 36 chains contained Secret information at the time; and eight contained Confidential information, which is the lowest level of classification."[37]

In other words, then-Secretary of State Hillary Clinton used a private, unsecured internet server (not a secure government server) to read and transmit various levels of classified documents across the internet. Further, Secretary Clinton decided which of her emails were relevant to the investigation, and which were not, deleting emails she claimed were not responsive to the request.

---

[35] Jon Greenberg, Politifact, "Comparing Hillary Clinton's emails and Donald Trump's boxes of files", August 9, 2022

[36] FBI.gov, "Statement by FBI Director James B. Comey on the Investigation of Secretary Hillary Clinton's Use of a Personal E-Mail System", July 5, 2016

[37] Ibid.

According to Comey, "[a]lthough we did not find clear evidence that Secretary Clinton or her colleagues intended to violate laws governing the handling of classified information, there is evidence that they were extremely careless in their handling of very sensitive, highly classified information. For example, seven e-mail chains concern matters that were classified at the Top Secret/Special Access Program level when they were sent and received. These chains involved Secretary Clinton both sending e-mails about those matters and receiving e-mails from others about the same matters. There is evidence to support a conclusion that any reasonable person in Secretary Clinton's position...should have known that an unclassified system was no place for that conversation. In addition to this highly sensitive information, we also found information that was properly classified as Secret by the U.S. Intelligence Community at the time it was discussed on e-mail...[n]one of these e-mails should have been on any kind of unclassified system, but their presence is especially concerning because all of these e-mails were housed on unclassified personal servers not even supported by full-time security staff, like those found at Departments and Agencies of the U.S. Government—or even with a commercial service like Gmail."[38]

Was this a criminal act? Under 18 USC 1924[a], "[w]hoever, being an officer, employee, contractor, or consultant of the United States, and, by virtue of his office, employment, position, or contract, becomes possessed of documents or materials containing classified information of the United States, knowingly removes such documents or materials without authority and with the intent to retain such documents or materials at an unauthorized location shall be fined under this title or imprisoned for not more than five years, or both."

Nonetheless, Comey claimed his investigation showed that Clinton and her staff did not "intend" to violate the law, and the applicable statute does require acting "knowingly" and "with intent". However, to be found guilty of a violation of this statute, you do not need to have intended to break the law - you need to have intended to retain the classified documents "at an unauthorized location." As discussed by Anthony Christina in *The Penn State Law Review*, "[t]o convict Clinton, it must be shown that she had knowledge that classified emails were contained on her private server. The most

[38] Ibid.

recent total by the State Department of their review of 30,000 Clinton emails indicates that at least 671 emails sent or received by Clinton contained classified information. This fact stands in stark contrast to the statement Clinton gave to reporters...when she said, 'I am confident that I have never sent nor received any information that was classified at the time it was sent and received.'"[39]

The conclusion is inescapable - if a "reasonable person" would know that almost 700 emails were classified, and had no place on an unsecured server, it would not be hard to establish that then-Secretary Clinton intended "to retain such documents or materials at an unauthorized location."

So, was Hillary Clinton arrested and prosecuted for this violation of the law? In his July 5, 2016 statement, then-FBI Director Comey predicted the outcome; "Although there is evidence of potential violations of the statutes regarding the handling of classified information, our judgment is that no reasonable prosecutor would bring such a case...In looking back at our investigations into mishandling or removal of classified information, we cannot find a case that would support bringing criminal charges on these facts." [40]

No reasonable prosecutor would bring such a case.... we cannot find a case that would support bringing criminal charges on these facts...

I guess James Comey missed this one then; "On April 23, [2015, General David] Petraeus pled guilty to a single misdemeanor charge of unauthorized removal and retention of classified documents or materials under 18 USC Sec. 1924...[i]nstead of turning his journals — so-called 'black books' - over to the Defense Department or CIA when he left either of those organizations, Petraeus kept them at his home - an unsecure location - and provided them to his paramour/biographer, Paula Broadwell, at another private residence."[41]

Did Gen. Petraeus "intend to break the law?" No - but he did intend to retain classified documents at an unsecured location and fail

[39] Anthony Christina, Penn State Law Review, "What Law Did Hillary Clinton Actually Break?" November 17, 2015

[40] FBI.gov, "Statement by FBI Director James B. Comey on the Investigation of Secretary Hillary Clinton's Use of a Personal E-Mail System", July 5, 2016

[41] Ken Cuccinelli, New York Post, "Yes, Hillary Clinton broke the law", September 27, 2015

to keep them secure.

Maybe Comey never heard of the Petraeus case - or maybe he thought the prosecutor was unreasonable.

One fact cannot be disputed - in 2016, Hillary Clinton was the Democratic candidate for President. David Petreaus was a Republican, though he "stresses his independence and has not voted for years."[42]

If you ask David Laufman who led the Justice Department's counterintelligence section until 2018 and is now a partner at the firm Wiggin and Dana, "[p]eople sling these cases around to suit their political agenda but every case has to stand on its own circumstances." While with the Justice Department, Laufman investigated the Clinton case, and managed the investigation of David Petraeus. Regarding the Trump investigation, Laufman believes that "[f]or the department to pursue a search warrant at Mar-a-Lago tells me that the quantum and quality of the evidence they were reciting — in a search warrant and affidavit that an FBI agent swore to — was likely so pulverizing in its force as to eviscerate any notion that the search warrant and this investigation is politically motivated."[43]

Maybe there is sufficient evidence to charge former-President Trump with a crime and bring criminal indictments against him. Maybe the prosecutions of the 45th President are not politically motivated. Maybe the cases of Petraeus, Clinton and Trump must each stand on their own merits.

But none of that explains why it's reasonable and appropriate to pursue charges against Republicans Petraeus and Trump, but not reasonable to seek the same against the Democrat Clinton.

---

[42] Phil Stewart, and Adam Entous, Reuters, "Five facts about General David Petraeus", June 24, 2010

[43] Kyle Cheney, Politico, "Why the Trump search warrant is nothing like Clinton's emails", August 9, 2022

2 AN OUTRAGEOUS ABUSE OF PROCESS

The right of the people to be secure in their persons, houses, papers, and effects, against unreasonable searches and seizures, shall not be violated, and no warrants shall issue, but upon probable cause, supported by oath or affirmation, and particularly describing the place to be searched, and the persons or things to be seized. Fourth Amendment, United States Constitution

Having served as a Criminal Court Judge in Brooklyn, New York, I had many occasions to hear evidence from witnesses, police officers and confidential informants, and to issue search warrants. In most cases, the police and an Assistant District Attorney would present me with a proposed search warrant and a supporting affidavit. A confidential informant (CI) would usually appear in person and would testify under oath as to the allegations contained in the supporting affidavit. The warrant would detail the place to be searched, and what items were expected to be found.

As is stated in the Fourth Amendment, a search warrant could not be issued until probable cause was established; that is, proof that a crime had occurred, and that specific evidence of that crime could be found at the location to be searched. For example, the CI would testify that he purchased drugs at a specific apartment on one or more occasions; and that the CI had observed that a drug "stash" was located in a cardboard shoe box in the living room of that apartment.

It was my job to ensure that such a warrant did not become a "fishing expedition", that is, just an open-ended search through a person's home for unspecified contraband. I had an obligation to establish parameters, such as a time period during which the warrant could be executed; whether or not the police had an obligation to knock first; and a requirement that the searching authorities return to the courthouse after the search with a list of the items seized.

For instance, in the example used above, the police could search the living room of the apartment, but not every bedroom at the location.

If the police found a safe, or other closed container in the course of their search, unless the warrant specified otherwise, the searching authorities could not enter that safe or closed container without seeking another warrant. Again, in the example given above, the search warrant would authorize the police to search any cardboard shoe box found in the living room of the apartment.

I also had the authority to change the search warrant by striking out provisions I did not wish to authorize or add terms I believed necessary. Further, I could also reject the entire warrant, or call for its resubmission with the alterations I would approve.

On August 8, 2022, a search warrant was executed by approximately 30 Agents of the Federal Bureau of Investigation's Washington DC bureau office at former President Donald Trump's residence in Florida, Mar-A-Lago. According to *The Guardian*, "[t]he search warrant appeared to be approved by Florida federal magistrate judge Bruce Reinhart. The attachment to the warrant, describing the 'property to be seized', broadly referred to classified documents and materials responsive to the Presidential Records Act."

Apparently, the search grew out of a months-long dispute between Trump and the National Archives. "In late January [2022], after protracted negotiations with Trump lawyers, the Archives secured the return of 15 boxes of documents Trump took from the White House to Mar-a-Lago, his post-presidency home in Florida. The boxes included White House documents considered presidential records, as well as items including "love letters" from Kim Jong-un of North Korea, a letter left for Trump by his predecessor as president, Barack Obama, and a model of Air Force One with red-white-and-blue livery Trump chose."[44]

Yet, the recovery of these materials wasn't enough for the National Archives, the Department of Justice, or the FBI. Further, rather than subpoena these documents, or seek a Court order for their return, federal authorities sought and obtained a search warrant.

"In executing the search warrant...teams of FBI agents wearing

---

[44] Hugo Lowell, The Guardian, "Trump improperly took away classified material, National Archives says", February 18, 2022

nondescript clothes fanned out across the entirety of the Mar-a-Lago resort in Palm Beach, Florida, the sources said. Trump was not there at the time of the raid and learned about it while he was in New York. The agents searched through storage areas in the basement of the property, the sources said, before moving to Trump's office on the second floor of the main house, where a safecracking team opened a hotel-style safe, though that contained no records responsive to the warrant. Later, the FBI agents searched the residence of Trump and his wife, Melania, and navigated through the pocket-door that separates their separate rooms, one of the sources said."[45]

In fact, as a result of the search, "sources said [approximately] 10 boxes' worth of documents [were recovered] in addition to 15 boxes recovered from Mar-a-Lago earlier this year." [46]

Given my background, and the rules for the issuance of search warrants I outlined above, several issues immediately jumped out at me.

First, as described in Chapter 3, below, the warrant used to search the President's residence is extraordinarily broad. "Classified documents and materials responsive to the Presidential Records Act," could mean any one of a thousand or more categories of material. Further, such a wide description gives FBI Agents no particular and specific description of the materials subject to the search.

Next, the area to be searched is not specified. Agents searched all of Mar-A Lago, including the private residence of the former President and his wife; the former President's office; and even a closed and locked safe. As will be discussed in Chapter 3, the warrant allowed for a very broad and far-ranging search, a highly unusual unspecific and wide mandate.

Third, as we have discussed, a court must find probable cause for a crime to have occurred to issue a search warrant. What is the crime here? Under 18 USC Sec. 2071[a], "Whoever willfully and unlawfully conceals, removes, mutilates, obliterates, or destroys, or attempts to do so, or, with intent to do so takes and carries away any record...document, or other thing, filed or deposited...in any public office, or with any judicial or public officer of the United States, shall

---

[45] Hugo Lowell, The Guardian, "FBI searched Trump's home seeking classified presidential record - sources", August 10, 2022

[46] Ibid.

be fined under this title or imprisoned not more than three years, or both." Subdivision (b) goes on to state that "[w]hoever, having the custody of any such record...document, paper, or other thing, willfully and unlawfully conceals, removes...or destroys the same...shall forfeit his office and be disqualified from holding any office under the United States."

According to former federal prosecutor Andrew McCarthy, writing in *The New York Post*, "If Trump had not declassified these materials while he was president, then his continuing possession of them in a non-secure location was probably illegal. While presidents have unilateral authority to declassify intelligence, they only maintain that authority while in office – it may not be exercised in the post-presidency. The returned documents were thus potentially evidence of crimes. In addition, since it is believed Trump did not return everything that was shipped out of the White House in those hectic days of January 2021, there was significant reason to suspect he continued to retain classified information at Mar-a-Lago."[47]

But as noted, the penalties for a violation of 18 USC Sec. 2071 are fairly minimal. Was it really necessary to send 30 FBI Agents from Washington DC to South Florida to search for 10 boxes of documents? Is there some other motivation for the government to have acted so ham-fistedly here?

As Andrew McCarthy writes, "there is speculation that DOJ may be mobilizing now in order to trigger Section 2071 disqualification. I doubt that. The Justice Department well knows that the qualifications for a presidential candidate are set out in the Constitution. They may not be altered by statute, precisely because the Framers did not want the executive branch to be dominated by the legislature, as would happen if Congress could disqualify incumbent or potential presidents simply by passing a law. The Constitution's qualifications for the presidency are minimal – one must be over 35 and a natural-born citizen. Being a felon is not a disqualification, so even crimes potentially far more serious than mishandling classified information are not a bar to seeking the presidency."[48]

As a result, McCarthy "believe it would [be] foolhardy for the Biden Justice Department to indict a former president on such

---

[47] Andrew McCarthy, New York Post, "Trump raid not about classified documents - it's about Jan 6", August 9, 2022

[48] Ibid.

debatable non-violent crime charges. That is especially so when it comes to a former president who will be the 2024 Republican nominee, since such charges would fuel the perception that Democrats are using the Justice Department as a political weapon." [49]

In fact, McCarthy believes the raid on Mar A Lago had another motive; "The Justice Department obviously used the potential classified information as a pretext to obtain a warrant so it could search for what it is really looking for: evidence that would tie Trump to a Capitol riot offense – either a violent crime, such as seditious conspiracy to forcibly attack a government installation (which is highly unlikely), or a non-violent crime, such as conspiracy to obstruct the January 6 joint session of Congress to count electoral votes, or conspiracy to defraud the government."[50]

This would explain the open-ended nature of the warrant, and the wide-ranging search throughout the former President's residence - a classic "fishing expedition." Exactly what an objective issuing magistrate is duty-bond to prevent.

Whatever the fall out, one thing is certain. No matter how you may view former President Trump, if the government can use a pretext like the retention of some documents as a predicate for a full-blown search of his property, what reliance can the rest of us have on the fairness and impartiality of our judges and magistrates?

---

[49] Ibid.

[50] Ibid.

3 AN OVERBROAD AND UNSPECIFIC EXPRESSION OF HATE

"Towards thee I roll, thou all-destroying but unconquering whale; to the last I grapple with thee; from hell's heart I stab at thee; for hate's sake I spit my last breath at thee." Captain Ahab, Moby Dick by Herman Melville.

It came as no surprise to anyone when Liz Cheney (R-WY) lost her primary to retain her seat as Wyoming's only Congressperson. "With 80% of the vote counted before midnight, [Harriet] Hageman was leading Cheney by more than 32 points."[51] The daughter of the former Vice President was doomed to lose her seat long before the primary election, when "[t]he Wyoming Republican Party voted...to censure Rep. Liz Cheney and also asked her to resign for her vote last month to impeach then-President Donald Trump after the insurrection at the Capitol on Jan. 6."[52]

But Liz Cheney won't give up her own hunt for the white whale. "Cheney told CBS News' Robert Costa that her primary loss is "certainly the beginning of a battle that is going to continue to go on"...[i]n her closing message, Liz Cheney made it clear that her focus remains squarely on Trump: 'The lie that the 2020 presidential election was stolen is insidious. It preys on those who love their country. It is a door Donald Trump opened to manipulate Americans to abandon their principles, to sacrifice their freedom, to justify

---

[51] Jonathan Allen, and Henry J. Gomez, NBC News, "Rep. Liz Cheney loses her primary in Wyoming to Trump-backed challenger", August 16, 2022

[52] John Ruwitch and Barbara Sprunt, NPR, "Wyoming GOP Censures Liz Cheney For Voting To Impeach Trump", February 6, 2021

violence, to ignore the rulings of our courts and the rule of law.'"[53]

Liz Cheney is only one example of our national leaders who have decided to spit their last political breaths at Donald Trump. The most obvious, and glaring example of this unreasonable hatred of the 45th President is the search warrant executed at Mar A Lago by 30 Agents from the Washington DC office of the FBI.

The Florida Federal Magistrate who signed the warrant, Bruce Reinhart, "attacked President Trump for his comments about former congressman and woke hero John Lewis...[i]n a Facebook post dated 14 January 2017 (before he was appointed a Magistrate), Reinhart [said] "Thank you, [former Labor Secretary] Robert Reich, for saying what many of us feel...John Lewis is the conscience of America. Donald Trump doesn't have the moral stature to kiss John Lewis's feet."[54]

Perhaps after his appointment, Magistrate Reinhart had repudiated these feelings about President Trump? Not according to Reinhart himself; "U.S. Magistrate Judge Bruce W. Reinhart in West Palm Beach, Fla...recused himself from the former president's lawsuit against Hillary Clinton and other Democrats in the Russia collusion scandal, citing concerns he couldn't be impartial...'[t]he undersigned Magistrate Judge, to whom the above-styled cause has been assigned, hereby recuses himself and refers the case to the Clerk of Court for reassignment pursuant to 28 USC Sec. 455,"[55] Reinhart wrote in his order of recusal in the *Trump v. Clinton* case.[56]

"The statute that the magistrate cited for his recusal states in part that a judge 'shall disqualify himself in any proceeding in which his impartiality might reasonably be questioned' and then describes the various circumstances that could trigger such concerns. They include 'a personal bias or prejudice concerning a party, or personal knowledge of disputed evidentiary facts' or prior work as a lawyer for a party involved in the case. Reinhart's order did not specify the

---

[53] Aaron Navarro, CBS News, "Liz Cheney says 'it's the beginning the battle' ahead of Republican primary loss", August 17, 2022

[54] Allum Bokhari, Breitbart, "Facebook Posts Reveal Epstein-Linked Magistrate Bruce Reinhart's Woke, Anti-Trump Attitudes", Augugst 10, 2022

[55] John Solomon, The Ohio Press Network, "BREAKING: Judge who authorized Mar-a-Lago search previously recused self from Trump-Clinton lawsuit", August 10, 2022.

[56] Donald J. Trump v. Hillary Clinton, Case No. 22-14102, Notice of Recusal, United States District Court, Southern District of Florida, June 22, 2022.

conflict or source of his concern for recusal."[57]

The Recusal Order is dated June 22, 2022. Six weeks later, on August 5, 2022, Magistrate Reinhart signed the search warrant for Mar A Lago. Did his concern that his "impartiality might reasonably be questioned" evaporate in that time?

A reading of the search warrant indicates otherwise.

Magistrate Reinhart's warrant authorizes a search of "1100 S Ocean Blvd, Palm Beach, FL 33480...described as a resort, club, and residence located near the intersection of Southern Blvd and S Ocean Blvd. It is described as a mansion with approximately 58 bedrooms, 33 bathrooms, on a 17-acre estate. The locations to be searched include the '45 Office,' all storage rooms, and all other rooms or areas within the premises used or available to be used by FPOTUS and his staff and in which boxes or documents could be stored, including all structures or buildings on the estate. It does not include areas currently (i.e., at the time of the search) being occupied, rented, or used by third parties (such as Mar-a-Largo Members) and not otherwise used or available to be used by FPOTUS and his staff, such as private guest suites."[58]

Note the very broad area to be searched - "all storage rooms...all other rooms or areas within the premises used or available to be used by [former President Trump]...all structures or buildings on the estate." Pretty much covers the whole place, doesn't it?

Equally broad is the description of the items to be searched for: "All physical documents and records constituting evidence, contraband, fruits of crime, or other items illegally possessed in violation of 18 USC Secs. 793, 2071, or 1519, including the following: a) Any physical documents with classification markings, along with any containers/boxes (including any other contents) in which such documents are located, as well as any other containers/boxes that are collectively stored or found together with the aforementioned documents and containers/boxes; b) Information, including communications in any form, regarding the retrieval, storage, or transmission of national defense information or classified material; c)

[57] John Solomon, The Ohio Press Network, "BREAKING: Judge who authorized Mar-a-Lago search previously recused self from Trump-Clinton lawsuit", August 10, 2022

[58] In Re Sealed Search Warrant, Case No. 22-MJ-8332-BER, United States District Court, Southern District of Florida, filed August 11, 2022

Any government and/or Presidential Records created between January 20, 2017, and January 20, 2021, or d) Any evidence of the knowing alteration, destruction, or concealment of any government and/or Presidential Records, or of any documents with classification markings."[59]

A list of what items weren't covered by this warrant would have been shorter.

Blinded by his hatred of Donald Trump, perhaps Judge Reinhart forgot that a search warrant must identify a *specific* place to be searched, and *particular* items to be seized. "The Fourth Amendment [to the United States Constitution] itself identifies the criteria for obtaining a lawful search warrant. A police officer, or other official seeking a warrant...must 'particularly describ[e] the place to be searched, and the persons or things to be seized.' *A search warrant is invalid if it covers too broad an area or does not identify specific items or persons.*" (Emphasis added).[60]

As noted in the case of *United States v. Galpin*, 720 F3d 436 (2nd Circuit, 2013), "The chief evil that prompted the framing and adoption of the Fourth Amendment was the 'indiscriminate searches and seizures' conducted by the British 'under the authority of 'general warrants'...[t]o prevent such 'general, exploratory rummaging in a person's belongings' and the attendant privacy violations...the Fourth Amendment provides that 'a warrant may not be issued unless probable cause is properly established and the scope of the authorized search is set out with particularity'...the Supreme Court has held that the particularity requirement 'makes general searches ... impossible and prevents the seizure of one thing under a warrant describing another. As to what is to be taken, nothing is left to the discretion of the officer executing the warrant'...we have emphasized that 'a failure to describe the items to be seized with as much particularity as the circumstances reasonably allow offends the Fourth Amendment because there is no assurance that the permitted invasion of a suspect's privacy and property are no more than absolutely necessary.'" (Citations omitted).[61]

Following these general principles, and reviewing the extremely

---

[59] Ibid.

[60] Anonymous, Justia.com, "The Search Warrant Requirement in Criminal Investigations & Legal Exceptions", October 2023

[61] United States v. Galpin, 720 F3d 436 (2d Cir 2013)

broad language of the search warrant quoted above, it is obvious that Magistrate Reinhart authorized a "fishing expedition" at Mar A Lago, when he should have [a] recused himself from hearing the warrant application, as he did six weeks earlier from another matter in which Donald Trump was involved, (b) limited the search location and items to be searched for, or (c) reject the search warrant all together as overbroad.

Only someone who bears unreasoning hatred for the 45th President can justify a search so repugnant to the standards established by the Fourth Amendment. Someone like Liz Cheney. Or Magistrate Bruce Reinhart.

Much blame for this violation of the former President's rights can be assigned to the Department of Justice and the Federal Bureau of Investigation. However, the court which issues the search warrant is the gatekeeper, sworn to uphold the Constitution and ensure that the rights of the accused are protected and respected.

In this respect, Magistrate Reinhart has utterly failed at his job. Instead of maintaining impartiality and respect for the requirements of the law, Bruce Reinhart joined the hunt.

"*Aye, aye! and I'll chase him round Good Hope, and round the Horn, and round the Norway Maelstrom, and round perdition's flames before I give him up.*" Captain Ahab, Moby Dick by Herman Melville.

4 JOE BIDEN'S GARAGE OF SECRETS

As we discussed in Chapters 2 and 3, on August 8, 2022, the FBI executed a search warrant at the Florida residence of former President Donald Trump. At the time, Trump stated "My beautiful home, Mar-A-Lago in Palm Beach, Florida, is currently under siege, raided, and occupied by a large group of FBI agents."[62] The search was intended to recover documents housed at Trump's residence that the National Archives claimed did not belong in the former President's hands.

As is well known, a series of documents labeled "classified" were recovered from Mar-A-Lago pursuant to the search.[63]

Current President Joe Biden wasted no time in criticizing his predecessor. "When it emerged President Trump had so many top secret documents in his possession, Biden asked: '...how that could possibly happen? How anyone could be that irresponsible? What data may be in there that may compromise sources and methods?'"[64]

Perhaps Joe Biden never heard the phrase, "People who live in glass houses shouldn't throw stones."

On November 2, 2022, "President Biden's personal attorneys unexpectedly discover[ed] Obama-Biden administration records at the Penn Biden Center in Washington, and notif[ied] the National

---

[62] Kaitlan Collins, et al., CNN, "FBI executes search warrant at Trump's Mar-a-Lago in document investigation", August 9, 2022

[63] Rema Rahman, The Hill, "Trump held more than 300 classified documents after leaving White House: report", August 22, 2022

[64] Mark Stone, Sky News, "One man's gaffe, another man's gift? What we know about the Biden classified documents discovery", January 12, 2023

Archives." On December 20, 2022, "Biden's personal attorneys inspect[ed] [the] garage at the president's Wilmington [Delaware] home and identif[ied] a 'small number' of potential classified records." Then, on January 11, 2023, "Biden's personal attorneys search[ed] the president's homes in Wilmington and Rehoboth Beach for additional records. They located a potential record with classified markings in a room adjacent to the garage."[65]

The majority of the documents recovered from these offices and residences appear to date from Biden's time as Vice-President.[66]

"People close to the White House say there is currently a mood of quiet resignation among Biden aides – an 'It is what it is' mentality – as they, too, wait to learn if news of more misplaced classified documents will surface in the coming days...Democratic Sen. Debbie Stabenow said the discovery of the classified documents was 'certainly embarrassing' for Biden. 'It's one of those moments that, obviously, they wish hadn't happened,' Stabenow said on NBC's 'Meet the Press.'"[67]

"It is what it is?" "Certainly embarrassing?" "Wish hadn't happened?"

Compare these understatements from Biden supporters with the rock thrown through Biden's glass house by Peter Doocy of *Fox News* after the second batch of documents were found in Biden's garage - "Classified materials next to your Corvette? What were you thinking?" All Biden could answer was "that the garage had been locked and that he took the proper handling of classified documents seriously."[68]

Other than Doocy's direct question, the rest of the media has been very understanding of Biden's incompetent handling of classified materials. According to "Scott Amey, general counsel for the Project on Government Oversight, 'I'd bet you that if they go back to all of the living presidents and root through their homes and

---

[65] Kevin Liptak, CNN, "What we know about the Biden classified documents: A timeline of events" January 16, 2023

[66] Gangel, Jamie, Cohen, Marshall, Perez, Ethan and Mattingly, Phil, CNN, "Classified documents from Biden's time as VP discovered in private office", January 9, 2023

[67] M.J. Lee and Kevin Liptak, CNN, "'Unforced errors': A White House facing a fresh crisis", January 16, 2023

[68] William Gittens, AS, "Biden pressed by Fox News' Peter Doocy over classified documents found in his garage", January 12, 2023

their libraries and their warehouses and garages, they're going to unearth some classified documents there'...Such security lapses are a somewhat regular occurrence, according to one former senior security official involved in protecting classified presidential documents under Trump and his predecessor, Barack Obama...Mark Zaid, a lawyer who specializes in the handling of classified information, said such lapses date back to World War II or earlier, and are far more common than is known publicly."[69]

Sure, no big deal. Happens all the time.

But if Biden's mishandling of classified documents is a routine matter, why was it necessary to use dozens of FBI Agents with a search warrant to recover documents from Donald Trump that "all living presidents" have in their homes, libraries, and garages?

According to *Sky News*, there are three main differences between Trump's and Biden's situations: "Firstly, quantity. Fewer than twelve documents were found at the Penn Biden Center and "a handful" were found in Delaware. More than 160 were found at Mar-a-Lago. This excuse might not hold water: one document in the wrong hands could be one too many. Secondly, location. In relation to the first batch of Biden documents discovered, it's arguable that a private office-space is distinct from a personal home which doubles as a country club [Mar-a-Lago]. But then the second batch was found in President Biden's garage alongside, as it happens, his Corvette! The key difference between the two cases is intent. It's not unusual when someone at the top of government leaves office to find cases where documents of a secret nature get mixed up with those of a personal nature."[70]

All three of these alleged differences cannot withstand scrutiny.

As we discussed in Chapter 2, "[u]nder 18 USC 2071[a], 'Whoever willfully and unlawfully conceals, removes, mutilates, obliterates, or destroys, or attempts to do so, or with intent to do so takes and carries away any record...document, or other thing, filed or deposited...in any public office, or with any judicial or public officer of the United States, shall be fined under this title or imprisoned not more than three years, or both.'" Further, as we noted in Chapter 1,

---

[69] Josh Meyer, USA Today, "Biden and Trump documents expose wider problem: Missing classified records not uncommon", January 19, 2023

[70] Mark Stone, Sky News, "One man's gaffe, another man's gift? What we know about the Biden classified documents discovery", January 12, 2023

"[u]nder 18 USC 1924[a], '[w]hoever, being an officer, employee, contractor, or consultant of the United States, and, by virtue of his office, employment, position, or contract, becomes possessed of documents or materials containing classified information of the United States, knowingly removes such documents or materials without authority and with the intent to retain such documents or materials at an unauthorized location shall be fined under this title or imprisoned for not more than five years, or both.'" There is no "it's only a couple of pages" defense, nor is there a "private-office space" distinction from a "personal home" in either of these statutes. In fact, as *Sky News* admits, it is irrelevant how many documents are involved, or where they were kept. Possession of the documents outside of a secured location *itself* is the crime.[71]

Therefore, we are left with intent as the crucial issue. But the legal standard for "willfully and unlawfully...removes" and "intent to retain such documents...at an unauthorized location" is not the same as the dictionary definition of those words. As we discussed in our review of Hillary Clinton's mishandling of classified materials, "to be found guilty of a violation of [these laws], you do not need to have intended to break the law – you need to have intended to retain the classified documents 'at an unauthorized location.' As discussed by Anthony Christina in *The Penn State Law Review*, '[t]o convict Clinton, it must be shown that she had knowledge that classified emails were contained on her private server. The most recent total by the State Department of their review of 30,000 Clinton emails indicates that at least 671 emails sent or received by Clinton contained classified information...[t]he conclusion is inescapable – if a 'reasonable person' would know that almost 700 emails were classified, and had no place on an unsecured server, it would not be hard to establish that then-Secretary Clinton intended 'to retain such documents or materials at an unauthorized location.'"[72]

To understand this distinction, let's review several cases where the Justice Department has prosecuted people for mishandling classified materials.

As recently as 2022, "[a] former civilian employee of the Defense Department was sentenced...to three months in prison after

[71] Ibid.

[72] Anthony Christina, Penn State Law Review, "What Law Did Hillary Clinton Actually Break?" November 17, 2015

admitting to taking materials containing classified information to her hotel room and to her personal residence...[t]he ex-Defense Department employee...Asia Janay Lavarello, was on a temporary assignment at the US Embassy in Manilla when she took classified documents from the embassy to her hotel room, according to court filings. She hosted a dinner party at her hotel on the day she removed the documents, March 20, 2020, and an embassy co-worker in attendance found the documents, which had classified markings on them, according to the court filings...The documents she took home were three...classified theses, her lawyer told CNN, and she had no intention of transmitting the classified information or of harming the United States."[73]

In 2013, "[r]etired Lieutenant Colonel Benjamin Pierce Bishop was arrested in Hawaii and charged with one count of unlawfully retaining documents related to the national defense...Court papers alleged Bishop, who was working for a defense contractor, stored 12 documents containing classified information at his residence."[74]

Then there is this case we described in Chapter 1; "On April 23, 2015, [General David] Petraeus pled guilty to a single misdemeanor charge of unauthorized removal and retention of classified documents or materials under 18 USC Sec. 1924…[i]nstead of turning his journals — so-called 'black books' – over to the Defense Department or CIA when he left either of those organizations, Petraeus kept them at his home – an unsecure location – and provided them to his paramour/biographer, Paula Broadwell, at another private residence.' Did General Petraeus 'intend to break the law?' No – but he did intend to retain classified documents at an unsecured location and fail to keep them secure."[75]

In each of these cases, it did not matter whether the defendant kept the classified documents in a private residence, a hotel, or any other location. The fact that the location was not *authorized* is the key factor.

Thus, it doesn't matter whether Biden kept those documents in

---

[73] Tierney Sneed, CNN, "Amid scrutiny of Trump White House docs, DOJ secures prison term for ex-Defense employee who mishandled classified materials", February 11, 2022

[74] Jeff Seldin, VOA News, "FBI, Justice Department Routinely Prosecute Misuse of Classified Documents", August 9, 2022

[75] Ken Cuccinelli, New York Post, "Yes, Hillary Clinton broke the law", September 27, 2015

his garage, his residence, or an office at the University of Pennsylvania. It matters that all of those places are "unauthorized location[s]."

Further, the number of documents is equally irrelevant. Lieutenant Colonel Bishop only had 12 documents; Ms Lavarello had 3; yet both still faced criminal prosecution.

Most important, however, intent does not mean, "I purposely broke the law." It means you intended to remove the documents from an authorized location and keep them at an unauthorized location. Like your office at the University of Pennsylvania. Or your garage, next to your Corvette. Or your residence.

In this regard, Trump may actually have a better argument in his behalf than Biden. According to CNN, "[i]n early June, a handful of investigators made a rare visit to the property seeking more information about potentially classified material from Trump's time in the White House that had been taken to Florida. The investigators asked the attorneys if they could see where Trump was storing the documents. The attorneys took the investigators to the basement room where the boxes of materials were being stored, and the investigators looked around the room before eventually leaving. Five days later, on June 8, Trump's attorneys received a letter from investigators asking them to further secure the room where the documents were stored. Aides subsequently added a padlock to the room."[76]

A locked room in a basement may not be an authorized location, but it's certainly more secure than any of the locations where the Biden documents have been discovered. In fact, investigators went to Mar-A-Lago, saw where the documents were stored, and only suggested that a lock be placed on the door. This potentially could be deemed a tacit authorization of the location where Trump was storing these documents.

In fact, the unsecured and unauthorized nature of the Biden home in Wilmington is underscored by the activities of the President's son, Hunter; "President Biden's formerly crack-addicted son described spending four days inside his father's 6,850-square-foot residence with other family members as they awaited the results of the 2020 presidential election...[he] described the family 'curled up on the couch

[76] Kaitlan Collins et al., CNN, "FBI executes search warrant at Trump's Mar-a-Lago in document investigation", August 9, 2022

together' with other relatives 'filtering in and out' as returns trickled in...Hunter...added that his parents weren't even home when the networks finally called the election for his father."[77]

Further, "[p]hotographs from 2017 obtained from Hunter Biden's abandoned laptop show the president's son in the driver's seat of his father's 1967 Chevrolet Corvette Stingray convertible, which the president says was kept in a 'locked garage' alongside classified documents from his time as vice president."[78]

There is one other argument that stands in former President Trump's favor; his power to declassify documents while serving as President. According to the American Bar Association, "most national security legal experts dismissed the former president's suggestion that he could declassify documents...[b]ut...legal guidelines support his contention that presidents have broad authority to formally declassify most documents that are not statutorily protected, while they are in office."[79]

While the ABA also asserts that "[i]n all cases...a formal procedure is required so governmental agencies know with certainty what has been declassified," there is little legal authority to support this view. The one case cited by the ABA, *New York Times v. CIA,* states that "[d]eclassification cannot occur unless designated officials follow specified procedures." However, the President of the United States, and a "designated official" are not necessarily the same. In fact, as the ABA admits, "the extent of a president's legal authority to unilaterally declassify materials — without following formal procedures — has yet to be challenged in court."[80]

As discussed in *The Hill*, "it would be wrong to simply dismiss Trump's assertion...Presidents have long claimed the authority to classify materials by dint of the president being the nation's chief executive and commander in chief - the only official vested under Article II of the Constitution with 'the executive power.' Any other official involved in classifying materials does so, it is argued, because the president has delegated that authority to that official. And

---

[77] Victor Nava, New York Post, "Hunter Biden wrote he 'quarantined' at Delaware house where classified documents were stored", January 19, 2023
[78] Ibid.
[79] Anonymous, American Bar Association, ABA News, "Fact check explores presidential authority to declassify", October 24, 2022
[80] Ibid.

because the president has the underlying power to classify, he has by implication the unilateral authority to declassify."[81]

Whether Biden, as Vice President, could have declassified the documents found in his possession is not as clear-cut; "A March 2003 executive order signed by President George W. Bush empowered the vice president to classify sensitive materials. That same executive order grants declassification powers to 'the official who authorized the original classification' or 'a supervisor official.' Under the executive order, vice presidents are granted the power to declassify documents they classified themselves. But it's unclear if the vice president would be viewed as 'a supervisory official' with the ability to declassify sensitive documents from the CIA and other intelligence agencies. That leaves it muddled whether a vice president can declassify documents."[82]

In any event, Biden doesn't claim he declassified anything. Instead, "President Biden said...he was 'surprised' to learn...that his lawyers found classified government documents in his former office at a think tank in Washington, and he said he does not know what information they contain."[83]

Apparently, Joe Biden has never heard another old adage - "Ignorance of the law is no excuse."

On January 12, 2023, Attorney General Merrick Garland appointed Special Counsel Robert Hur to investigate "the possible unauthorized removal and retention of classified documents or other records discovered at the Penn Biden Center for Diplomacy and Global Engagement and the Wilmington, Delaware, private residence of President Joseph R. Biden Jr."[84] Hur is the former US Attorney for Maryland, and according to *The Associated Press*, "Hur was principal associate attorney general under [Rod] Rosenstein at the Justice Department. Hur is also a former partner at the Washington law firm King & Spalding, where FBI Director Christopher Wray was once also a partner."[85]

---

[81] Gary Schmitt and Henry Sokolski, The Hill, "Don't dismiss Trump's assertion of presidential power to declassify information", December 23, 2022

[82] Jeff Mordock, The Washington Times, "Discovery of Biden documents sparks debate over vice president's declassification powers", January 10, 2023

[83] Glenn Thrush and Charlie Savage, The New York Times, "Biden 'Surprised' to Learn Classified Documents Were Found in Private Office", January 9, 2023

[84] Press Release, US Department of Justice, "Appointment of a Special Counsel", January 12, 2023

Remember Rod Rosenstein from our Introduction? He signed off on the FISA warrants, which were based on the Steele Dossier. Then, he appointed Robert Mueller as Special Counsel to investigate the "Russian collusion" allegations that also turned out to be false.

These associations do not mean that Hur will not conduct an honest investigation. But to date, he has certainly conducted a slow moving one. It wasn't until October of 2023 that Hur interviewed the current President in person, a move which PBS believes "could signal that the special counsel investigation is nearing its conclusion."[86]

In fact, according to former federal prosecutor Jonathan Turley, "[u]nlike his counterpart, Special Counsel Jack Smith, who has been aggressively prosecuting former president Donald Trump, Hur has virtually disappeared since his appointment to investigate President Joe Biden."[87]

Indeed. Contrast the speed with which Smith moved with the lack of progress to date in Hur's investigation. Is this equal justice, equally applied?

---

85 Will Weissert, AP News, "Who is Robert Hur, special counsel in Biden documents case?", January 12, 2023

86 Darlene Superville and Eric Tucker, PBS, "Biden interviewed as part of special counsel investigation into handling of classified documents", October 9, 2023

87 Jonathan Turley, The Hill, "New evidence may destroy Biden's defense in his classified documents case", October 14, 2023

5 "A MAN SHOULD BE HUNG FOR WHAT HE'S DONE, NOT FOR WHAT HE AIN'T DONE."

Daniel Keith was a notorious con man and swindler in Rutherford County, North Carolina. "His biggest swindle took place in 1879 when he took a sixty-eight-pound rock and rubbed it with brass. He sold this 'gold' mine to many men in Western Carolina making him one of the most unpopular men in North Carolina. Many swore that they would get even with him; and in January of 1880, a tragedy would give them the opportunity to rid Rutherford County of Daniel Keith once and for all."[88]

That year, a young girl was found brutally raped and murdered. Suspicion fell on Keith when "a witness came forth and said that he had seen Daniel Keith in the area and that he appeared to be drunk and belligerent. A couple of hours later Sheriff [NE] Walker contacted Keith at his cabin. He was sober, but there were bloodstains on his shirt. The Sheriff asked him where the stains had come from, and Keith stated that he had 'been skinning rabbits.' His story was not believed even though the carcasses of the rabbits had been found. Keith was arrested [and] was found guilty...in spite of evidence produced in the trial that there was an escaped convict from neighboring McDowell County who had been sighted in the area by several persons. This fugitive had been awaiting execution for the same [type of] crime [of which] Keith was accused."[89]

After having the appeal of his conviction denied, Keith "professed

---

[88] Pat Mendoza, Remember Cliffside, "The Legend of Daniel Keith", undated

[89] Ibid.

his innocence up to the moment" he was hanged, saying, among other things, "a man should be hung for what he's done, not for what he ain't done."[90]

As we noted in our Introduction, there can be no doubt that former President Donald Trump is a very polarizing figure. There seems to be no middle ground with Trump - you either hate him, or you love him. Unfortunately, the people who hate the former President the most are currently in power.

One of those who clearly "has it out" for Trump is Manhattan District Attorney Alvin Bragg. While campaigning for the office he currently holds, Bragg "repeatedly touted his experience suing Trump...while serving as the state's chief deputy attorney general from 2017 to 2018, leading to the shutdown of the Donald J. Trump Foundation and payment of $2 million in court-ordered damages...following his election, Bragg, who took office Jan. 1, 2022, again invoked his experience suing Trump in response to the stunning resignations of prosecutors Mark Pomerantz and Carey Dunne, who had led the Trump investigation until clashing with their new boss."[91]

According to the *Atlantic News Telegraphic*, "[n]o, Bragg did not specifically pledge, 'If elected, I will indict Donald J. Trump.' But he promised to pursue Trump and hold him 'accountable,' which is progressive code for going after Trump in any way possible."[92]

No one can say that Alvin Bragg isn't a man of his word. As is well known, on March 30, 2023, a Manhattan Grand Jury voted to Indict former President Trump for 34 counts of Falsifying Business Records in the First Degree, a violation of NY Penal Law Section 175.10.[93] On April 4, 2023, Trump was arraigned in New York County Supreme Court on this indictment and entered a plea of Not Guilty.[94]

---

[90] Ibid.

[91] Bruce Golding, New York Post, "DA Bragg's looming indictment of Trump follows campaign trail boasts", March 23, 2023

[92] Byron York, Atlantic News Telegraph, "For Prosecutor Bragg, Trump Indictment is a Campaign Promise Kept", April 10, 2023

[93] People of the State of New York v. Donald J. Trump, IND-71543-23, Supreme Court, State of New York, County of New York, Indictment and Statement of Facts, Dated April 4, 2023

[94] Jeremy Herb, Kara Scannell, and Lauren del Valle, CNN, "Donald Trump pleads not guilty to 34 felony counts of falsifying business records", April 4, 2023

Let us put aside the unprecedented nature of these events, that is, the fact that a local District Attorney has brought state criminal charges against a former President of the United States for the first time in the history of our nation. Let us also ignore (for now) the emotional arguments from both left and right as to whether Trump is a martyr, being prosecuted for trying to "drain the swamp" of Washington DC politics, or a villain like Daniel Keith, someone who deserves to go to jail (or even be executed) for something, anything, just so long as he is stopped.

Instead, let us consider this case as if Trump were any other defendant accused of a crime. Objectively speaking, are there facts sufficient to substantiate the charges brought against Donald Trump?

One of the first steps any criminal defense lawyer would take in defense of any client is an examination of the indictment for legal sufficiency. Under Section 200.50 of the New York State Criminal Procedure Law, "an indictment must contain...[a] statement in each count that the grand jury...accuses the defendant...of a designated offense," as well as "[a] plain and concise factual statement in each count which... asserts facts supporting every element of the offense charged and the defendant`s...commission thereof with sufficient precision to clearly apprise the defendant...of the conduct which is the subject of the accusation."

According to the first count of the indictment, "[t]he defendant, in the County of New York and elsewhere...with intent to defraud and intent to commit another crime and aid and conceal the commission thereof, made and caused a false entry in the business records of an enterprise, to wit, an invoice from Michael Cohen dated February 14, 2017, marked as a record of the Donald J. Trump Revocable Trust, and kept and maintained by the Trump Organization."[95] Each of the rest of the charges all involve different documents on different dates, but each contains the exact same phrase; "with intent to defraud and intent to commit another crime and aid and conceal the commission thereof."

This language would appear to track the language of New York Penal Law Section 175.10, which states that "a person is guilty of falsifying business records in the first degree...when his intent to

[95] People of the State of New York v. Donald J. Trump, Ind-71543-23, Supreme Court, State of New York, County of New York, Indictment and Statement of Facts, April 4, 2023

defraud includes an intent to commit another crime or to aid or conceal the commission thereof."

Thus, under Count One of the Indictment, Donald Trump is accused of causing a false entry to be made in one of the business records of his Revocable Trust for the purpose of committing another crime.

"Another crime." What other crime? The indictment does not say - and herein lies a very elemental problem for the Manhattan District Attorney.

As we noted above, New York law requires an indictment to "assert facts supporting every element of the offense charged," the "defendant's commission thereof," and to assert those facts "with sufficient precision to clearly apprise the defendant of the conduct which is the subject of the accusation."

These are basic requirements under New York State's criminal law. In the 2018 case of *People v. Ramcharran*, the Queens County Criminal Court wrote that "[t]o be facially sufficient, an accusatory instrument must specify the offense[s] charged and contain factual allegations of an evidentiary nature that tend to support them...[s]uch factual allegations...must consist of non-hearsay allegations that provide reasonable cause to believe that the defendant committed the offense[s] charged, which if true, establish each and every element of those charges... mere conclusory allegations are insufficient...[i]t must...at a minimum, provide an accused with adequately detailed factual allegations of an evidentiary nature sufficient for a defendant to prepare a defense, and prevent him from being tried twice for the same offense." (Citations omitted.)[96]

Simply put, how is former President Trump to prepare a defense, if he is not informed of the "other crime" he intended to commit or conceal when he allegedly falsified his business records?

Certainly, the law does allow the District Attorney to supplement the Indictment with an additional statement of facts, such as a Bill of Particulars. But unless the prosecution amends the indictment itself, the document which accuses Trump of a crime is clearly and substantially insufficient on its face.

The *Ramcharran* case involved the District Attorney's failure to include the right location where the crime was allegedly committed in

---

[96] People v. Ramcharran, New York City Criminal Court, Queens County, 2018 WL 3553300 (Kirschner, J), July 19, 2018

the indictment, which is another potential defect in the Trump indictment - note that the location of the crime is stated to be "the County of New York and *elsewhere*" (emphasis added). Here, notice of the actual crime which was allegedly violated by former President Trump is missing, a far more serious omission.

Trump's defense counsel will undoubtedly file a motion asking the judge to inspect the minutes of the District Attorney's presentation of the case to the Grand Jury, "for the purpose of determining whether the evidence before the grand jury was legally sufficient to support the charges" under CPL Sec. 210.30.

If the Grand Jury was not informed of the "other crime" which Trump intended to commit or conceal when he allegedly falsified his business records (or where "elsewhere" is located), then the presentation to the Grand Jury was hopelessly, fundamentally flawed, and the indictment must be dismissed.

Will this indictment be dismissed, on this, or any other basis? Frankly, don't hold your breath waiting. The judge assigned the case, Juan Merchan, has already handled two other matters brought against the Trump Organization, both of which resulted in criminal convictions.[97]

This, in and of itself, does not make Merchan unfair or biased. However, according to *The New York Post*, Merchan "donated $35 to Democratic causes in 2020, including $15 to President Biden's campaign and $10 to a group dedicated to 'resisting … Donald Trump's radical right-wing legacy.'"[98]

Does this record of political donations sound like someone who would dismiss Alvin Bragg's indictment against Donald Trump?

[97] Jennifer Peltz, and Michael R. Sisak., AP News, "Who is Juan Merchan, the NY judge handling Trump's case?", April 3, 2023

[98] Victor Nava, New York Post, "Judge Juan Merchan, who is overseeing Trump case, donated to Biden campaign in 2020", April 7, 2023

6 IS TRUMP'S NEW YORK STATE INDICTMENT BEYOND THE STATUTE OF LIMITATIONS?

In Chapter 5, we discussed the glaringly obvious facial insufficiency of the Manhattan District Attorney's Indictment of former President Donald Trump. We noted that Trump was charged with 34 counts of Falsifying Business Records in the First Degree, a Class E felony under New York's Penal Law Section 175.10.

Each count of the indictment states that Trump, "with intent to defraud and intent to commit another crime and aid and conceal the commission thereof, made and caused a false entry in the business records of an enterprise."[99] We noted that the failure to specify the "other crime" at issue renders the indictment facially insufficient since it does not "provide an accused with adequately detailed factual allegations of an evidentiary nature sufficient for a defendant to prepare a defense and prevent him from being tried twice for the same offense."[100]

In and of itself, as we argued in Chapter 5, the failure to present sufficient factual allegations should be enough to allow the Court to dismiss the indictment. But there is another basis upon which the prosecution of Donald Trump could be rendered untenable.

A review of the indictment reveals that the criminal acts alleged

---

[99] People of the State of New York v. Donald J. Trump, Ind-71543-23, Supreme Court, State of New York, County of New York, Indictment and Statement of Facts, Dated April 4, 2023

[100] People v. Ramcharran, New York City Criminal Court, Queens County, 2018 WL 3553300 (Kirschner, J), July 19, 2018

occurred on a variety of dates between February 14, 2017 and December 5, 2017. Yet, Donald Trump was not arraigned on these charges until April 4, 2023 - more than six years after the events happened. Under New York Criminal Procedure Law Sec. 30.10(2)(b), "[a] prosecution for any other felony must be prosecuted within five years after the commission thereof."

Trump himself asserted that the Statute of Limitations had passed in a tweet from March of 2023.[101] Lawyer Tom Crist, writing for *The Federalist* agrees; "the D.A. had to bring...any felony charge in 2022 to survive a defense motion to dismiss. Bragg's grand jury handed up charges in 2023 after the five-year limitations period expired...the time for Bragg to charge Trump for the crimes listed in the indictment expired months or years ago and can no longer be pursued."[102] Of course, as with almost any law, there are exceptions and extensions available to Bragg's office.

One such argument for an extension of time can be made under CPL Sec. 30.10(4), which states that "in calculating the time limitation applicable to commencement of a criminal action, the following periods shall not be included: [a] Any period following the commission of the offense during which (i) the defendant was continuously outside this state or (ii) the whereabouts of the defendant were continuously unknown and continuously unascertainable by the exercise of reasonable diligence."

According to *CNN*, "[s]ince Trump was sworn into office in January 2017, he has spent few days in New York, which means prosecutors could effectively add that time to the clock and investigate earlier conduct."[103] *The Daily Beast* agrees; "Trump's time in the White House and his post-presidential political exile at the Mar-a-Lago estate in Florida may be gifting prosecutors much-needed extra time...Adam Kaufmann, an attorney who ran the Manhattan DA's investigative unit for three years [said] 'it's easy to prove he was not in the state of New York. There's going to be

---

[101] Wills Robinson, Daily Mail, "Trump claims the statute of limitations has ALREADY passed in Stormy Daniels case - as his ally Robert Costello prepares to testify against Michael Cohen to grand jury with ex-President bracing for charges", March 20, 2023

[102] Tom Crist, The Federalist, "Yes, The Statute Of Limitations Has Passed On Bragg's 'Get Trump' Case", April 10, 2023

[103] Kara Scannell, CNN, "Trump's time in White House could end up benefiting New York prosecutors", March 12, 2021

records of where he was physically located every day for four years.'"[104]

Attorney Crist does not think much of any effort to apply this exception to the former president: "CNN has been telling us since 2021, two years before Bragg's indictment of the former president, that the time Trump spent in the White House would be tacked on to the New York statute of limitations to keep the prospect of criminal charges against Trump alive. Other networks have mimicked that conclusion. Each has focused on the contention that any period following the commission of the offense during which a defendant resided outside of New York will serve to extend the statutory time bar...Trump was front-page news for his entire presidency. He was not hiding from anyone. He did not evade Bragg. He loves and lives in the limelight...Trump routinely visited New York City over the last several years and maintains at least one home and business assets there. If Bragg could not figure out where Trump was from 2016 to 2022, he has bigger problems than this weak indictment."[105]

Reasonable minds would tend to agree with Crist's analysis here. Trump was not making any effort to hide from the Manhattan DA's office and its investigation from 2016 to 2023. He maintained a residence in New York City during his presidency, and only recently established a Florida residency. Even then, he was in and out of New York continuously during that time period.

But the former president is not dealing with reasonable minds. Further, as described by *CNN*, there is precedent for the use of the extension period of CPL Sec. 30.10(4); "The [Manhattan] district attorney's office invoked the out-of-state tolling extension in its criminal case against [Hollywood producer Harvey] Weinstein. Prosecutors charged Weinstein with multiple crimes, including rape in the third degree for an alleged assault that occurred in March 2013. Weinstein was charged in May 2018, two months after the five-year statute of limitations on that offense would have expired. Weinstein challenged the charge, arguing it fell outside the statute of limitations and as a non-resident of New York state the extension wouldn't apply to him. Prosecutors used records from "United States Customs and Border Control" to show that

---

[104] Jose Paglieri and Asawinr Suebsaeng, The Daily Beast, "The Obscure Law NY Prosecutors Could Use to Charge Trump Years From Now", April 12, 2022

[105] Tom Crist, The Federalist, "Yes, The Statute Of Limitations Has Passed On Bragg's 'Get Trump' Case", April 10, 2023

Weinstein had been out of New York for 193 days during that five-year period– more than the 68 days needed to capture the earlier conduct. The judge rejected Weinstein's argument and allowed the charge to stand. Weinstein was convicted on charges of sexual assault and is serving a 23-year sentence."[106]

Thus, it is entirely possible that the time Donald Trump spent in the White House, serving his country as the President of the United States, could be used against him in New York State Supreme Court.

There is also another issue that could allow for the extension of the time period for at least some of the charges brought against the former president.

On March 20, 2020, then-New York Governor Andrew Cuomo issued Executive Order No. 202.8, which reads in part, "any specific time limit for the commencement, filing, or service of any legal action, notice, motion, or other process or proceeding, as prescribed by the procedural laws of the state, including but not limited to the criminal procedure law, the family court act, the civil practice law and rules, the court of claims act, the surrogate's court procedure act, and the uniform court acts, or by any other statute, local law, ordinance, order, rule, or regulation, or part thereof, is hereby tolled from the date of this executive order until April 19, 2020…"[107] This "toll" of the "time limit for the commencement...of any legal action" was continually extended until November 3, 2020, a total of approximately 8 months, or 228 days.[108]

What does this mean? In 2021, New York State's Appellate Division, Second Department, in the case of Brash v. Richards, considered the question of "whether a series of executive orders issued by Governor Andrew Cuomo, as a result of the COVID-19 pandemic, constitute a toll...of filing deadlines applicable to litigation in the New York courts." The Court concluded "that the subject executive orders constitute a toll of such filing deadlines."[109]

---

[106] Kara Scannell, CNN, "Trump's time in White House could end up benefiting New York prosecutors", March 12, 2021

[107] Governor Andrew Cuomo, Executive Order No. 202.8, "Continuing Temporary Suspension and Modification of Laws Relating to the Disaster Emergency", March 20, 2020

[108] Governor Andrew Cuomo, Executive Order No. 202.67, "Continuing Temporary Suspension and Modification of Laws Relating to the Disaster Emergency", October 4, 2020

[109] Brash v. Richards, 195 AD3d 582 (2d Dept, 2021)

The Court explained that "[a] toll suspends the running of the applicable period of limitation for a finite time period, and '[t]he period of the toll is excluded from the calculation of the [relevant time period].'" (Citation omitted.)[110] As described by New York attorney Krystina Maola, "[s]hould the remaining appellate courts follow the holding in *Brash* and decide the Executive Orders were meant as a toll of filing deadlines, this would extend filing deadlines for a period of 228 days...Therefore, any statute of limitations that was set to expire on November 3, 2020 (the last day the Executive Orders provided for tolling) will now expire on June 19, 2021." (Citation omitted.)[111]

To understand the effect this tolling of the statute of limitations has on the Trump indictment will require a bit of math. On average, the five years between 2017 and 2023 would add up to approximately 1,825 days. Meanwhile, the time between December 5, 2017 (the last date of criminal conduct alleged against Trump) and the former president's arraignment on April 4, 2023, is 1,946 days. This would mean that Trump's arraignment occurred 121 days past the five-year expiration of the statute of limitations.

However, if we subtract the 228 days of the toll period (between March 20 and November 3, 2020) from those 1,946 days, we get 1,718 days. That's 108 days short of the five-year expiration date.

These 108 days do not save all of the prosecutor's charges. The first 22 counts of the indictment, which allege acts which occurred between February 14, 2017 and August 1, 2017 are more than five years old, even given the Governor's tolling order. Only Counts 23 through 34, which allege illegal acts which occurred between September 11, 2017 and December 5, 2017 would not be time barred under this analysis.

This means that some, but not all of the charges brought by the Manhattan DA's Office could be dismissed under this theory.

In any event, as we discussed in Chapter 5, the New York County Supreme Court justice hearing this matter is Juan Merchan, who has previously contributed to anti-Trump political organizations.[112] The

[110] Ibid.

[111] Krystina Maola, Gallo Vitucci Klar, LLP, "Covid Related Executive Orders and their effect on the Statute of Limitations in New York", June 21, 2021

[112] Victor Nava, New York Post, "Judge Juan Merchan, who is overseeing Trump case, donated to Biden campaign in 2020", April 7, 2023

likelihood of a dismissal of any charges on any basis by Judge Merchan is low. Instead, as stated by *Vox*, "we may need to wait a very long time before the courts determine once and for all whether Trump may be convicted under the felony statutes he is accused of violating — indeed, if the [United States] Supreme Court gets involved in this case, we may not get an answer until well after the 2024 election. And, of course, even if Bragg does convince the courts that Trump was properly charged with a felony, he will still need to prove that case to a jury beyond a reasonable doubt."[113]

In other words, as we stated in Chapter 5, don't hold your breath waiting for Donald Trump to receive any dismissal of any charges by the trial court.

---

[113] Ian Millhiser, Vox, "The dubious legal theory at the heart of the Trump indictment, explained", April 4, 2023

7 TRUMP'S NEW YORK STATE INDICTMENT BREAKS NEW LEGAL GROUND

In Chapter 5, we discussed the facial insufficiency of the Indictment brought against former President Donald Trump in Manhattan Supreme Court In particular, we noted that "[u]nder Section 200.50 of the New York State Criminal Procedure Law, 'an indictment must contain…[a] statement in each count that the grand jury…accuses the defendant…of a designated offense,' as well as '[a] plain and concise factual statement in each count which… asserts facts supporting every element of the offense charged and the defendant`s…commission thereof with sufficient precision to clearly apprise the defendant…of the conduct which is the subject of the accusation.'"

Regarding this issue, we noted that each count of the Trump Indictment "contains the exact same phrase; 'with intent to defraud and intent to commit another crime and aid and conceal the commission thereof'…[t]his language would appear to track the language of NY Penal Law Section 175.10, which states that 'a person is guilty of falsifying business records in the first degree…when his intent to defraud includes an intent to commit another crime or to aid or conceal the commission thereof.'"

No where does the Indictment identify the "other crimes" that Donald Trump was allegedly attempting to conceal when he falsified his business records. On this basis alone, we argued that the Indictment is insufficient, and must be dismissed, since Trump is not properly advised of which law he allegedly broke, and cannot adequately prepare a defense.

This issue, however, is only the tip of the iceberg of a much broader basis for a potential dismissal of Trump's Indictment.

Falsifying Business Records in the First Degree is a Class E felony, the lowest level of felony offense under New York State law. Meanwhile, Falsifying Business Records in the Second Degree is only a Class A misdemeanor. The Second Degree charge only requires an "intent to defraud" when a person "[m]akes or causes a false entry in the business records of an enterprise," while the First Degree requires the additional step of doing so with "an intent to commit another crime or to aid or conceal the commission thereof."

This is a very important distinction between the felony charges brought against former President Trump, and the misdemeanor charges not brought. Under New York's Criminal Procedure Law Section 30.10, a prosecution for a Class E felony must be brought within five years after the commission of the crime. A Class A misdemeanor must be brought within two years of the commission of the crime alleged.[114]

In Chapter 6, we discussed the application of the Statute of Limitations to the felony charges brought against the former President. We stated that "[a] review of the indictment reveals that the criminal acts alleged occurred on a variety of dates between February 14, 2017 and December 5, 2017. Yet, Donald Trump was not arraigned on these charges until April 4, 2023 - more than six years after the events happened." We also noted that there are several "tolls" or extensions of the five year time period for the prosecution of a criminal charge - one being CPL Sec. 30.10(4), which states that "in calculating the time limitation applicable to commencement of a criminal action, the following periods shall not be included: [a] Any period following the commission of the offense during which (i) the defendant was continuously outside this state or (ii) the whereabouts of the defendant were continuously unknown and continuously unascertainable by the exercise of reasonable diligence."

Thus, we noted that "it is entirely possible that the time Donald Trump spent in the White House, serving his country as the President of the United States, could be used against him in New York State Supreme Court."

We also discussed the tolling of the Statute of Limitations due to a

[114] New York Criminal Procedure Law Section 30.10 (2021)

series of Executive Orders signed by former New York Governor Andrew Cuomo, which halted the running of the time to bring any legal action in New York State from March 20, 2020 to November 3, 2020, a total of approximately 8 months, or 228 days. Yet, as we also noted, this toll would not save all 34 counts of the Trump Indictment since at least the first 22 counts are beyond the time period affected by the toll.

But let us return to the underlying issue to be discussed in this chapter- what are the "other crimes" that makes this a felony prosecution, instead of a time-barred misdemeanor?

Besides the Indictment, the Manhattan District Attorney's Office also filed a Statement of Facts with the Manhattan Supreme Court. According to this document, "the Defendant [Donald Trump] orchestrated a scheme with others to influence the 2016 presidential election by identifying and purchasing negative information about him to suppress its publication and benefit the Defendant's electoral prospects. In order to execute the unlawful scheme, the participants violated election laws and made and caused false entries in the business records of various entities in New York. The participants also took steps that mischaracterized, for tax purposes, the true nature of the payments made in furtherance of the scheme." [115]

In other words, the former President tried to influence a presidential election in which he was a candidate by suppressing negative information about himself. But as stated by James Bovard in *The New York Post*, "[d]oes Manhattan prosecutor Alvin Bragg believe political campaigns are governed by the Boy Scout oath and every candidate must be honest, trustworthy, clean and maybe reverent, too?... Lyndon Johnson won in 1964 because he deceived Americans about the Gulf of Tonkin resolution and his plans to plunge into war in Vietnam. Richard Nixon won in 1972 in part because Americans had not heard his Oval Office tapes exposing the cover up of the Watergate break-in. President Barack Obama was re-elected in 2012 in part because Americans did not know about the vast illegal National Security Agency spying operation that Edward Snowden exposed the next year. Does anyone expect President Joe Biden to open federal files to expose his debacles during his re-election

[115] People of the State of New York v. Donald J. Trump, Ind-71543-23, Supreme Court, State of New York, County of New York, Indictment and Statement of Facts, April 4, 2023

campaign? 'Suppressing negative information' is standard operating procedure in Washington."[116]

Bovard's point is well taken; but to be honest, it's not the suppression of negative information that is the alleged crime - it's the method used to cover up the payments.

According to the Statement of Facts, "at the Defendant's request, a lawyer who then worked for the Trump Organization as Special Counsel to Defendant ("Lawyer A"), covertly paid $130,000 to an adult film actress shortly before the election to prevent her from publicizing a sexual encounter with the Defendant. Lawyer A made the $130,000 payment through a shell corporation he set up and funded at a bank in Manhattan. This payment was illegal, and Lawyer A has since pleaded guilty to making an illegal campaign contribution and served time in prison. Further, false entries were made in New York business records to effectuate this payment, separate and apart from the New York business records used to conceal the payment."[117]

"Lawyer A" is clearly former Trump attorney Michael Cohen, who, in August of 2018, "pleaded guilty to eight counts in federal court in New York...[t]hey include five counts of tax evasion, one count of falsifying submissions to a bank and two counts involving unlawful campaign contributions...[t]he counts related to campaign finance violations involved payments that were made to keep two women quiet during the [2016 Presidential] campaign...Cohen was 'repaid at the direction of the candidate [Donald Trump]...with invoices for 'services rendered.' As described by Robert Khuzami, deputy U.S. attorney for the Southern District of New York at the time of Cohen's guilty plea, those "invoices were a sham...merely reimbursement for illegal campaign contributions."[118]

What is important to notice here; Cohen plead guilty to *federal* charges, relating to *federal* election law violations, which are alleged to have occurred in the course of a *federal* election.

Turing again to the Statement of Facts, more details emerge

[116] James Bovard, The New York Post, "Bragg's fairy-tale indictment pretends politicians never suppress embarrassing info", April 5, 2023

[117] People of the State of New York v. Donald J. Trump, Ind-71543-23, Supreme Court, State of New York, County of New York, Indictment and Statement of Facts, April 4, 2023

[118] Ryan Lucas and Tamara Keith, NPR, "Donald Trump's Attorney And Fixer Michael Cohen Pleads Guilty To 8 Federal Counts", August 21, 2018

regarding the nature of the "illegal campaign contributions"; "After the [2016 Presidential] election, the Defendant [Donald Trump] reimbursed Lawyer A [Michael Cohen] for the illegal payment through a series of monthly checks, first from the Donald J. Trump Revocable Trust (the 'Defendant's Trust')—a Trust created under the laws of New York which held the Trump Organization entity assets after the Defendant was elected President—and then from the Defendant's bank account. Each check was processed by the Trump Organization, and each check was disguised as a payment for legal services rendered in a given month of 2017 pursuant to a retainer agreement. The payment records, kept and maintained by the Trump Organization, were false New York business records. In truth, there was no retainer agreement, and Lawyer A was not being paid for legal services rendered in 2017. The Defendant caused his entities' business records to be falsified to disguise his and others' criminal conduct."[119]

In other words, Trump is alleged to have reimbursed "Lawyer A" (Michael Cohen) for the "illegal campaign contributions" Cohen made (that is, the "hush money" payments), and then falsified his own business records to disguise these reimbursement payments as "payment for legal services rendered" by Cohen to Trump.

Let us suppose that categorizing Trump's payments to Cohen as "reimbursement for legal services rendered" is a falsification of the business records of the Trump Organization. That could fit the definition of Falsifying Business Records in the Second Degree - the Class A misdemeanor - "makes or causes a false entry in the business records of an enterprise." But we are still left with one crucial question - where is the "intent to commit another crime or to aid or conceal the commission thereof" that makes these acts a felony under Falsifying Business Records in the First Degree?

According to a Statement issued by Manhattan District Attorney Alvin Bragg right after Donald Trump's arraignment, "The People of the State of New York allege that Donald J. Trump repeatedly and fraudulently falsified New York business records to conceal crimes that hid damaging information from the voting public during the 2016 presidential election... as the Statement of Facts describes, the

---

[119] People of the State of New York v. Donald J. Trump, Ind-71543-23, Supreme Court, State of New York, County of New York, Indictment and Statement of Facts, April 4, 2023

trail of money and lies exposes a pattern that, the People allege, violates one of New York's basic and fundamental business laws."[120]

Putting this statement together with the Statement of Facts leads us to only one conclusion - the "other crime" which elevates the charge against Trump from a misdemeanor to a felony, is a violation of *federal* campaign finance laws, for actions taken in the course of the 2016 Presidential election.

This leads us to another question - does the District Attorney of Manhattan, elected to serve one of the five boroughs of New York City, have the authority, the jurisdiction, to prosecute a violation of federal election law? Even if that underlying federal crime serves only to support a New York State criminal charge being elevated from a misdemeanor to a felony?

Even *CNN* has its doubts about a federal charge serving as the basis for a state charge. "Exactly what this underlying crime was is not specified in the indictment itself, but rather teased in an accompanying statement of facts and in prosecutors' remarks...[t]hey describe an 'unlawful' scheme to influence the 2016 election by keeping damaging information about Trump from reaching the public. The district attorney's theory, as well as the lack of transparency around how Bragg intends to lay it out, is raising concern about whether the case will stand up in court. Election law expert Rick Hasen told *CNN* it was "far from a slam dunk...[i]t raises some political questions whether this is the case to bring,' said Hasen, a professor at UCLA School of Law." Hasen also told CNN that he was "'skeptical' that a federal campaign finance prosecution could be used to back charges in a state court."[121]

According to Ian Millhiser writing at *Vox*, "Bragg built his case on an exceedingly uncertain legal theory. Even if Trump did the things he's accused of, it's not clear Bragg can legally charge Trump for them, at least under the felony version of New York's false records law. As Mark Pomerantz, a former prosecutor in the Manhattan DA's office who played a significant role in the Trump investigation prior to his resignation in 2022 wrote in a recent book, a

---

120 Anonymous, Manhattan District Attorney's Office, Press Release, "District Attorney Bragg Announces 34-Count Felony Indictment of Former President Donald J. Trump", April 4, 2023

121 Tierney Sneed, CNN, "Why New York's hush money case against Donald Trump is viewed as risky", April 5, 2023

key legal question that will determine whether Trump can be charged under the felony version of New York's false records law has never been resolved by any appellate court in the state of New York. The felony statute requires Bragg to prove that Trump falsified records to cover up a crime. Bragg has evidence that Trump acted to cover up a *federal* crime, but it is not clear that Bragg is allowed to point to a federal crime in order to charge Trump under the New York state law. The answer to this 'gnarly legal question,' as Pomerantz put it, is simply unknown."[122]

Whether DA Bragg can prove the charges brought against former President Trump is another issue, for consideration on another day. For now, the fundamental question presented here is whether a local prosecutor can use an alleged (and to date, unspecified) violation of federal election law as the basis for an elevation of a state criminal charge from a misdemeanor (that would be time-barred from prosecution), into a felony.

With that question in mind, let us give the last word on this matter to George Washington University law professor Jonathan Turley. In a *Fox News* interview broadcast shortly after the indictment, Turley said that "[Bragg] is attempting to bootstrap [a] federal crime into a state case. And if that is the basis for the indictment, I think it's rather outrageous...I think it's illegally pathetic."[123].

---

[122] Ian Millhiser, Vox, "The dubious legal theory at the heart of the Trump indictment, explained", April 4, 2023

[123] Steven Nelson, The New York Post, "Democrats giddy at Trump indictment, but legal experts warn case is weak", April 3, 2023

8 THE FIRST FEDERAL INDICTMENT

"I'm the most fun, I'm rich, and I'm always in trouble." Larry Flynt, quoted in *The People v. Larry Flynt* (1996)

Comparing former President Donald Trump with pornographer Larry Flynt (best known for publishing the utterly raunchy *Hustler* magazine) can lead to certain...misunderstandings. But both have some attributes in common - and Flynt summed up those similarities in the quote above.

In the 1970's and 1980's, Flynt was involved in a series of lawsuits, including "[h]is most famous legal case [which] involved [the Reverend] Jerry Falwell, founder of [The] Moral Majority. In 1983, Hustler ran a liquor advertisement parody suggesting that Falwell had lost his virginity to his mother in an outhouse. Falwell sued, saying he suffered emotional distress. In *Hustler Magazine v. Falwell* (1988), the Supreme Court invalidated a lower court's $200,000 damage award and ruled that a public figure cannot recover damages stemming from a satirical attack. The decision demonstrated that the adult entertainment industry is frequently in the vanguard of First Amendment free speech court battles that affect the wider culture."[124]

Much like Flynt, who died in 2021, Trump is not afraid to use his money to defend himself from various allegations and charges. In doing so, Trump ends up a leader in protecting the rights of others. Also similar to Flynt, Trump appears to relish a fight. As noted by *NBC News*, "Donald Trump gets up every day ready to face whatever

---

[124] Caryn E. Neumann, Free Speech Institute, "Larry Flynt", September 19, 2023

comes at him. He doesn't think about yesterday and he doesn't worry about tomorrow. The fight before him is what he is focused on."[125] "In a sick way I sort of enjoy it" Trump said while speaking at the North Carolina Republican Party's convention in Greensboro, North Carolina this June.[126]

Still, no matter how much one enjoys a good fight, no one seriously enjoys defending oneself against a federal indictment. Trump had enough trouble on his plate regarding his indictment by the Manhattan District Attorney Alvin Bragg for allegations involving election fraud. Now, Special US Attorney Jack Smith has filed a 38-count indictment in the Southern District of Florida against the former President and one of his aides, Waltine Nauta.[127]

The allegations stem from the allegedly classified documents recovered by the FBI after their raid of Mar a Lago in the summer of 2022. As readers of Chapters 2 and 3 will no doubt remember; "a search warrant was executed by approximately 30 Agents of the Federal Bureau of Investigation's Washington DC bureau office at former President Donald Trump's residence in Florida...[a]ccording to *The Guardian*, '[t]he search warrant [was] approved by Florida federal magistrate judge Bruce Reinhart. The attachment to the warrant, describing the 'property to be seized', broadly referred to classified documents and materials responsive to the Presidential Records Act.'"[128]

In Chapter 2, we noted the overbroad nature of the search warrant used by the FBI; "Classified documents and materials responsive to the Presidential Records Act, could mean any one of a thousand or more categories of material. Further, such a wide description gives FBI Agents no particular and specific description of the materials subject to the search. Next, the area to be searched appears not to have been specified. Agents searched *all* of Mar-A Lago, including the private residence of the former President and his

---

[125] Reed Galen, NBC News, "Trump loves a good fight more than anything else. And his opponents are unwilling or unable to get on his level", July 1, 2018

[126] Aaron Kliegman, Fox News, "Trump reveals his thoughts on barrage of legal charges, investigations: 'In a sick way I sort of enjoy it'", June 10, 2023

[127] United States v Donald J. Trump, et. al., Indictment No. 23 CR 80101, United States District Court, Southern District of Florida, June 8, 2023

[128] Hugo Lowell, The Guardian, "FBI searched Trump's home seeking classified presidential record - sources", August 10, 2022

wife; the former President's office; and even a closed and locked safe."

We have also discussed the requirements for searches and seizures under the Fourth Amendment to the US Constitution; "a search warrant must identify a *specific* place to be searched, and *particular* items to be seized. 'The Fourth Amendment...itself identifies the criteria for obtaining a lawful search warrant. A police officer, or other official seeking a warrant…must 'particularly describ[e] the place to be searched, and the persons or things to be seized.' *A search warrant is invalid if it covers too broad an area or does not identify specific items or persons.'* (Emphasis added)."

Thus, before we begin any discussion of the indictment, it must be clearly understood that the search warrant used to obtain the materials used against the former President is seriously and fatally flawed.

What is the effect of the use of an illegal search warrant on a prosecution? "You might know that evidence the cops find during an illegal search of you or your belongings is probably inadmissible in criminal court...[g]enerally speaking, the prosecution can't use evidence that comes directly from police illegality—the seized object or the statement. But oftentimes, it also can't use evidence that derives from the illegality—something the officers discovered as a result of the object or statement. The latter is commonly referred to as the 'fruit of the poisonous tree.'"'[129]

The "fruit of the poisonous tree" doctrine was discussed extensively in the 1963 US Supreme Court case, *Wong Sun v. United States.* There Justice William Brennan ruled for the majority that "[i]n order to make effective the fundamental constitutional guarantees of sanctity of the home and inviolability of the person...this Court held nearly half a century ago that evidence seized during an unlawful search could not constitute proof against the victim of the search...The exclusionary prohibition extends as well to the indirect as the direct products of such invasions...[this] exclusionary rule has traditionally barred from trial physical, tangible materials obtained either during or as a direct result of an unlawful invasion." (Citations omitted.)[130]

---

[129] Michael Tarleton, Nolo, "Fruit of the Poisonous Tree: Illegally Obtained Evidence", undated

[130] Wong Sun v. United States, 371 US 471 (1963)

Like any other resident of the United States, Donald Trump is entitled to the protection of the United States Constitution. Further, it is undisputed that the warrant used to search his home lacked the specificity required by the Fourth Amendment to that Constitution. Therefore, that warrant MUST be ruled invalid, and the evidence seized during the search of the former President's residence *MUST* be suppressed.

No other result is possible if the Federal Courts follow the law.

A review of the Federal Indictment shows that the first 31 Counts all involve individual charges for 31 separate, allegedly classified documents recovered during the search of Mar a Lago. If the Court follows the well-established precedent of *Wong Sun* and applies the exclusionary rule, these documents must be suppressed, and the first 31 counts of the indictment would need to be dismissed as lacking supporting evidence.

Count 32 alleges a Conspiracy to Obstruct Justice by various witnesses who claim that Trump and his co-defendant made untrue statements regarding the location and/or existence of the allegedly classified documents and caused boxes of these documents to be moved around Mar a Lago. Count 33, (Withholding a Document or Record), is also predicated on similar conduct described in Court 32, as are Count 34 (Corruptly Concealing a Document or Record), Count 35 (Concealing a Document in a Federal Investigation), Count 36 (Scheme to Conceal), Count 37 and Count 38 (False Statements and Representations). All seek to use statements and/or actions taken by Trump and his co-defendant to allegedly "hide and conceal documents from a federal grand jury," "conceal boxes that contained documents with classification markings," and "make a materially false, fictitious and fraudulent statement and representation...during a grand jury investigation" regarding the existence and/or location of these documents.[131]

As to these counts, the exclusionary rule may or may not be applied. Returning to the *Wong Sun* case, the named defendant made statements that the government sought to use against him. According to Justice Brennan, "Wong Sun's unsigned confession was not the fruit of that arrest and was therefore properly admitted at trial. On the evidence that Wong Sun had been released on his own

[131] United States v Donald J. Trump, et. al., Indictment No. 23 CR 80101, United States District Court, Southern District of Florida, June 8, 2023

recognizance after a lawful arraignment and had returned voluntarily several days later to make the statement, we hold that the connection between the arrest and the statement had 'become so attenuated as to dissipate the taint.'"[132]

Thus, it is entirely possible that some of the statements attributed to Trump and his co-defendant which occurred after the Mar a Lago search, while a grand jury was considering charges, could be seen as "attenuated" from the initial illegality of the search. However, it is equally possible that the use of these statements and actions against Trump and his co-defendant are all necessarily dependent upon the seized documents being admissible.

After all, it is hard to show a jury that a defendant obstructed an investigation, when you cannot show that jury the subject of that investigation - in other words, how do I know what Trump was trying to hide, if these documents are suppressed, and cannot be used at evidence at the trial?

This means that even if the evidence is suppressed, and only the first 31 counts of the indictment are dismissed, the prosecution may still have a difficult time proving their case for the remaining charges.

Have no doubt - Former President Trump will fight for his rights every step of the way.

And in doing so, Trump fights for the rights of all citizens against the government's use of excessive, unspecific search warrants.

[132] Wong Sun v. United States, 371 US 471 (1963)

9 A DISSECTION OF THE FIRST FEDERAL INDICTMENT

As is well known at this point, former President Donald Trump was indicted by a Federal Grand Jury and is currently facing a criminal trial for these charges in the Southern District of Florida.[133]

In general, this Indictment is predicated upon a search of Trump's Florida residence, Mar A Lago conducted by 30 FBI Agents from the bureau's Washington DC office, using a warrant obtained from a Florida Federal Magistrate. In Chapters 2 and 3, we discussed the reasons this search warrant is in violation of the Fourth Amendment's prohibition against general warrants.

In Chapter 8, we explained why this violation of the Fourth Amendment must lead to the suppression of all evidence obtained in the FBI's illegal and outrageous search of Mar A Lago. We also explained why the suppression of the allegedly classified documents seized during this illegal search would (and must) lead to the dismissal of most, if not all charges in the Indictment.

In this Chapter, we will discuss some more issues and problems relating to Special Counsel Jack Smith's Indictment.

The most obvious and glaring concern relates to the first 31 counts brought against former President Trump - that is, 31 separate violations of 18 USC Sec. 793(e). (Each count is predicated on an individual allegedly classified document recovered during the illegal search of Mar A Lago.) Also known as the Espionage Act, this

[133]United States v Donald J. Trump, et. al., Indictment No. 23 CR 80101, United States District Court, Southern District of Florida, June 8, 2023

statute reads as follows: "Whoever having unauthorized possession of, access to, or control over any document...map...or note relating to the national defense, or information relating to the national defense which information the possessor has reason to believe could be used to the injury of the United States or to the advantage of any foreign nation, willfully communicates, delivers, transmits or causes to be communicated, delivered, or transmitted, or attempts to communicate, deliver, transmit or cause to be communicated, delivered, or transmitted the same to any person not entitled to receive it, or willfully retains the same and fails to deliver it to the officer or employee of the United States entitled to receive it."

It is important to highlight this particular language of the statute; "the possessor has reason to believe [the information] could be used to the injury of the United States or to the advantage of any foreign nation."

The typical Indictment brought by the majority of prosecutors only give a bare bones description of the actions of the defendant that are in violation of the law. For instance, an Indictment charging a Murder would accuse the defendant of causing the death of the victim with the intent to cause that death, by firing a bullet into the heart of said victim. The indictment would not typically tell you the make and caliber of the gun, nor would it tell you whether or not the victim and defendant were known to each other prior to the shooting.

Here, Smith has provided us with what is known as a "talking" Indictment - that is, he gives us an extensive explanation of the facts upon which the Indictment is based. 27 pages of facts to be precise.

According to the Indictment, "As president, Trump had lawful access to the most sensitive classified documents and national defense information gathered and owned by the United States government...over the course of his presidency, Trump gathered...official documents and other materials in cardboard boxes...the classified documents Trump stored in boxes included information regarding defense and weapons capability of both the United States and foreign countries...the unauthorized disclosure of these classified documents could put at risk the national security of the United States..."[134]

[134] United States v Donald J. Trump, et. al., Indictment No. 23 CR 80101, United States District Court, Southern District of Florida, June 8, 2023

There are two instances described by Smith's Indictment regarding Trump's alleged disclosure of classified information. "In July 2021...during an audio-recorded meeting with a writer, a publisher and two members of his staff, none of whom possessed a security clearance, Trump showed and described a "Plan of Attack" that Trump said was prepared for him by the Department of Defense. Further, "[i]n August or September of 2021...Trump showed a representative of his political action committee who did not possess a security clearance a classified map related to a military operation..."[135]

Regarding the first disclosure, Trump allegedly called the "Plan of Attack" "highly confidential" and "secret." In the second instance, Trump allegedly said he should not be showing the PAC representative the map.

It should be noted that a review of the 31 documents which form the basis for each individual count does not clarify which documents are the basis for the two disclosures described earlier in the indictment. Not a single one of the documents is described as either a "Plan" or a "Map," although Number 11 is described as an "undated document concerning military contingency planning of the United States."[136]

Let us assume, for the sake of argument, that Trump did exactly what he is accused of doing - that he showed classified documents or maps to several individuals who did not possess a security clearance. Nonetheless, do either of these incidents as described in the Indictment fit the description of the state of mind necessary to be in violation of 18 USC Sec. 793(e), that is, "the possessor has reason to believe [the information] could be used to the injury of the United States, or to the advantage of any foreign nation"?

For instance, does the Indictment state that Trump expressed any intention to provide any foreign country with an advantage over the United States by disclosing this information? No, it does not. Does the Indictment state that Trump intended harm to the interests of the United States by his disclosure? Again, the answer is no.

Finally, is there any allegation that any of the persons who received this information did then provide that information to any

---

[135] Ibid.

[136] Ibid.

foreign nation, or make any effort to harm the United States and its interests? Once more, the answer is no. There is no allegation made in the Indictment that these individuals went on to either injure the United States or act to the advantage of any foreign nation.

According to the *BBC*, however, "[t]he part of the law referenced by the special counsel's indictment in Mr Trump's case...does not say that the suspect must be working with another country to deliberately harm the US... Under the law, prosecutors will not be required to prove that Mr Trump knew that the information he possessed could harm national security interests, but rather that any reasonable person would understand the harm it could do."[137]

Yet, this analysis is contradicted by reference to other people charged under the Espionage Act, such as Julius and Ethel Rosenberg, Jonathan Pollard, and Chelsea Manning - all spies, or at the very least, persons intent on harming the United States and giving an advantage to a foreign government.

In a time not so long ago, a prosecution under the Espionage Act caused concern among civil libertarians. As described by the National Constitution Center, "[t]hroughout American history, free speech has often been tested during times of war. During World War I, President Woodrow Wilson pushed for new laws that criminalized core First Amendment speech. Congress passed the Espionage Act shortly after the U.S. entered the war. The Act made it a crime to convey information intended to interfere with the war effort... [this law was] directed at socialists, pacifists, and other anti-war activists. The Wilson Administration argued that [this act was] essential to the war effort and prosecuted thousands of anti-war activists under their various provisions. While modern scholars view [the Espionage Act] as violating core free speech protections, the Supreme Court at the time upheld these convictions."[138]

Now it is mostly those on the political right who are troubled by the prosecution of former President Trump under the Espionage Act.

Another issue to be considered is brought up by former Acting US Attorney General Matthew Whitaker, who said "the interplay

---

[137] Max Matza, BBC, "If Trump isn't a spy, why is he being charged under the Espionage Act?", June 14, 2023

[138] Anonymous, National Constitution Center, "Espionage Act of 1917 and Sedition Act of 1918 (1917-1918)", undated

between the Presidential Records Act, which says all documents are covered by that act, and the Espionage Act...I think is going to be the most important issue that the courts are going to have to decide."[139]

In fact, the Presidential Records Act (PRA) of 1978, "established a... statutory structure under which Presidents...must manage the records of their Administrations... Specifically, the PRA.. Places the responsibility for the custody and management of incumbent Presidential records with the President... Requires that the President and his staff take all practical steps to file personal records separately from Presidential records....Establishes a process by which the President may restrict and the public may obtain access to these records after the President leaves office; specifically, the PRA allows for public access to Presidential records through the Freedom of Information Act (FOIA) beginning five years after the end of the Administration, but allows the President to invoke as many as six specific restrictions to public access for up to twelve years...[and] Codifies the process by which former and incumbent Presidents conduct reviews for executive privilege prior to public release of records."[140]

"After a presidency, the responsibility for the custody, control, preservation of, and access to presidential records shifts to the [National Archives]." However, significantly, "[t]he PRA does not provide the former President with a process for disposing of presidential records after leaving office."[141]

As most readers will recall, Trump was involved in extensive negotiations with the National Archives over which of his records were "Presidential" and which were "personal" when the debate was settled by the FBI and a search warrant. But charging the former President with a violation of the criminal Espionage Act, as opposed to suing him under the civil Presidential Records Act does not settle the matter.

To understand the difference, "let's examine the famous CLINTON SOCKS CASE...Key point: The case is not about Bill

---

139 Ashley Carnahan, Fox News, "Alan Dershowitz slams Trump indictment, shares one 'damning piece of evidence' in DOJ's case", June 11, 2023

140 National Archives, Presidential Libraries, "Presidential Records Act (PRA) of 1978"

141 Meghan M. Stuessy, EveryCRSReport.com, "The Presidential Records Act: An Overview", December 18, 2023

Clinton's cat named Socks...[r]ather, it involves tape recordings of conversations between President Clinton and historian Taylor Branch intended to serve as a personal diary of sorts, and which eventually formed the basis of Branch's 2009 book, "The Clinton Tapes." According to Branch, Clinton would store the tape recordings in his sock drawer for safekeeping and to ensure that staff didn't find, and possibly leak, the tapes. In 2010...Judicial Watch sued the National Archives and Records Administration (NARA), demanding that it obtain custody of the tapes and deposit them in the Clinton Presidential Library. Judicial Watch argued that Clinton should have included the tapes among the records transferred to NARA at the end of his presidency, and that NARA had to take steps to obtain the records. Judge Amy Berman Jackson dismissed the case because Judicial Watch did not identify anything that NARA could do to retrieve the tapes from Clinton. Jackson further noted that NARA was powerless to classify the records as presidential: '[T]he PRA does not confer any mandatory or even discretionary authority on the Archivist to classify records.'"[142]

Trump himself believes that the Presidential Records Act, and not the Espionage Act should be applied here. "Not only was Bill Clinton never even considered for criminal prosecution based on the tapes he took, but when he was sued for them, he won the case," the former President said in remarks made after his federal arraignment. "Judge Amy Berman Jackson's decision states: 'Under the statutory scheme established by the Presidential Records Act, the decision to segregate personal materials from Presidential records is made by the President during the President's term, and in the President's sole discretion'...[i]n other words, whatever documents a president decides to take with him, he has the right to do so. It's an absolute right. This is the law. And that is something that people have now seen and it couldn't be more clear. They ought to drop this case immediately."[143]

Naturally, it should be pointed out that Donald Trump is charged with more than just taking allegedly classified documents and declaring them to be personal records. He is also accused of making use of those supposedly classified records in at least two instances,

[142] Eric Columbus, Law Fare, "The Presidential Records Act, Clinton's Socks, and Trump's Boxes", June 21, 2023

[143] Hugh Allen, @rev, "Trump responds to charges in speech following arraignment in federal court transcript", June 14, 2023.

under circumstances where he had "reason to believe [the information] could be used to the injury of the United States or to the advantage of any foreign nation." But, if he is authorized to keep these documents under the PRA, whether marked "classified" or not, he is also authorized to make use of those documents as he wishes.

Though many legal minds do not believe the Presidential Records Act is applicable here, there are arguments which will have to be considered by a court before the matter could ever go to trial. In particular, as stated by Gregg Jarrett of *Fox News*, the PRA "granted an exclusive right of former presidents to maintain custody and control of presidential papers accrued during their terms in office. Arguably, it includes classified documents...[f]or more than a decade, it was the considered opinion of the Department of Justice that the PRA conferred a unique right on former presidents to keep whatever presidential records they want, and the government has no authority to seize them. The National Archives agreed. A president has the sole discretion to segregate and dispose of records...[f]orty-five years ago, Congress passed the Records Act to memorialize what previous presidents had always been permitted to do as a matter of tradition and practice. This is important since it is incumbent on courts to interpret statutes consistent with legislative intent. As The Wall Street Journal noted in a recent editorial, 'If the Espionage Act means Presidents can't retain any classified documents, then the PRA is all but meaningless.' Quite right."[144]

In other words, if the Court concludes that the Presidential Records Act, and not the Espionage Act is applicable to former President Trump's retention of all documents seized by the FBI in its raid at Mar A Lago, then the first 31 counts of the Indictment must be dismissed.

---

[144] Gregg Jarrett, Fox News, "Trump's indictment is not the slam dunk case liberal media believes it is", June 15, 2023

10 THE VIOLATION OF DONALD TRUMP'S RIGHT TO COUNSEL

In Chapter 8, we discussed the illegal search of Mar A Lago, and the necessity for the suppression of all evidence seized as illegally obtained "fruit of the poisonous tree." In Chapter 9, we examined the interaction between the Espionage Act, and the Presidential Records Act, as well as the potential defense that the former President had legal possession of the allegedly classified documents recovered during that illegal search and seizure.

In this chapter, we examine an extremely troubling aspect of this Indictment - the apparent violation of Donald Trump's right to counsel under the Sixth Amendment to the United States Constitution.

As is well known, the accused in every criminal matter has a right to counsel, and one important aspect of the relationship between an attorney and their client is known as the Attorney-Client Privilege. As described by Stephen M. Forte, Esq., the Managing Partner of Smith, Gambrell & Russell, LLP, "[t]he attorney-client privilege is the oldest privilege recognized by Anglo-American jurisprudence...[a]t its most basic, the privilege ensures 'that one who seeks advice or aid from a lawyer should be completely free of any fear that his secrets will be uncovered.' Thus, the underlying principle of the privilege is to provide for 'sound legal advice [and] advocacy.' With the security of the privilege, the client may speak frankly and openly to legal counsel, disclosing all relevant information to the attorney and creating a 'zone of privacy.' In other words, shielded by the privilege, the client may be more willing to communicate to counsel things that might otherwise be suppressed. In theory, such candor and honesty will assist the attorney in providing more accurate, well-reasoned professional advice, and the client can be secure in the knowledge that his statements to his lawyer will not be taken as an adverse admission or used against his interest." (Citations omitted.)[145]

Yet, if we review the June 2023 Indictment of former President Trump, we find these allegations:

"On May 23, 2022, Trump met with Trump Attorney 1 and Trump Attorney 2 at the Mar A Lago Club to discuss the response to the May 11 Subpoena [issued by the Justice Department]. Trump Attorney 1 and Trump Attorney 2 told Trump that they needed to search for documents that would be responsive to the subpoena...Trump, in sum and substance, made the following statements...as memorialized by Trump Attorney 1...'Well, what if we, what happens if we just don't respond at all or don't play ball with them?'...'Wouldn't it be better if we just told them we don't have anything here?'...Well look isn't it better if there are no documents?'"[146]

We also find these allegations as well; "Trump Attorney 1 located 38 documents with classification markings inside the boxes, which Trump Attorney 1 removed and placed in a Redwell folder...[a]fter Trump Attorney 1 finished sealing the Redwell folder...Trump and Trump Attorney 1 then discussed what to do with the Redwell folder...Trump made a plucking motion, as memorialized by Trump Attorney 1...'well okay why don't you take them with you to your hotel room and if there's anything really bad in there, you know, pluck it out'..."[147]

If respect is paid to the attorney-client privilege, then Trump is entitled to ask his lawyers any question he wants, and not have those questions used against him. Further, nowhere in the Indictment is "Trump Attorney 1's" response reported. More likely than not, "Trump Attorney 1" would have explained to the former President why documents would need to be produced in response to the Justice Department's subpoena. As Journalist Michael Tracey states, "'What happens if we just don't respond' is exactly the type of question you'd

[145] Stephen Forte, Smith, Gambrell Russell, LLP, "What the Attorney-Client Privilege Really Means", Issue 5, Fall 2003

[146] United States v Donald J. Trump, et. al., Indictment No. 23 CR 80101, United States District Court, Southern District of Florida, June 8, 2023

[147] Ibid.

expect a client to ask his lawyer in the context of privileged, confidential communications. But here the DOJ decided to 'seize' those communications and present them as evidence of criminal wrongdoing."[148]

But there is a more fundamental question that requires an answer - Where did Special Counsel Jack Smith get this information from in the first place? Obviously from "Trump Attorney 1," that is, Evan Corcoran, who was forced by the DC Circuit Court of Appeals "to testify and hand over records to special counsel Jack Smith's team investigating Trump's handling of classified records after leaving the White House."[149]

The higher court had been asked to overturn the order of D.C. District Judge Beryl Howell, who had "ruled that prosecutors in special counsel Jack Smith's office had made a 'prima facie showing that the former president had committed criminal violations,'" according to sources who described her...order, and that attorney-client privileges invoked by two of his lawyers, Corcoran and Jennifer Little, could therefore be pierced."[150]

But didn't we just review the nature of the Attorney-Client Privilege? What happened to the "zone of privacy" that allows a client to "be secure in the knowledge that his statements to his lawyer will not be taken as an adverse admission or used against his interest?"

As described by the Blog, *Above the Law*, "Judge Beryl Howell, in her last act as chief judge of the District Court in DC, found that the crime-fraud exception to attorney-client privilege applied to certain aspects of Corcoran's relationship with Trump, and she ordered him to testify to the grand jury investigating the wrongful retention of government documents at Mar-a-Lago. She also ordered him to hand over certain communications, including transcripts of recordings, immediately."[151]

---

[148] Chris Menahan, Information Liberation, "Jack Smith Setting 'Extraordinarily Dangerous' Precedent by Piercing Attorney-Client Privilege And Charging Trump 'For Asking a Question'", June 13, 2023

[149] Katherine Faulders and Alexander Mallin, ABC 7 Eyewitness News Chicago, "Appeals court rules Trump attorney Evan Corcoran must testify in special counsel's documents probe", March 22, 2023

[150] Ibid.

[151] Liz Dye, Above the Law, "DC Circuit Tells Trump Lawyer To Cough Up Docs To Special Counsel Under Crime-Fraud Privilege Exception", March 22, 2023

And just what is the "crime-fraud exception?"

"The attorney-client privilege does not cover statements made by a client to their lawyer if the statements are meant to further or conceal a crime. For this exception to apply, the client must have been in the process of committing a crime or planning to commit a crime...[s]ome of the crimes that often arise in this context include crimes that are meant to obstruct an investigation or ongoing prosecution...[a]n important distinction separates communications regarding a past crime from communications regarding an ongoing or future crime. The crime-fraud exception usually applies only to communications regarding ongoing or future crimes."[152]

This leads to the next question - what "ongoing or future crime" was being committed "to obstruct an investigation or ongoing prosecution?"

According to the June 2023 Indictment, the "obstruction" involved a certification made by Trump's Attorney's that a search of Trump's Records was conducted, and all that was found were the 38 pages turned over to the Justice Department, when in fact, Trump allegedly hid more documents in other Storage Boxes that were not searched by his lawyers.

The Indictment goes through a convoluted series of events that make it appear that Trump withheld some Storage Boxes from his attorneys, with the implication that this was done in an effort to lead Trump's counsel to make a false certification that all records responsive to the subpoena had been turned over to the Justice Department.

The indictment concludes by stating that the search of Mar A Lago revealed an additional 102 documents with varying degrees of classification. However, the Indictment does NOT state that these documents were recovered from any boxes which were allegedly kept from Trump's attorneys, nor is there a single word of explanation as to why the former President would want to turn over some classified documents to the Justice Department, but not others.

"It's rare that a court breaks attorney-client privilege, even rarer that the reason is that the lawyer was wittingly or unwittingly contributing to a crime or fraud," according to *The Bulwark*. "[w]hen Judge Beryl Howell told attorney Evan Corcoran that he had to

---

[152] Anonymous, Justia.com, "The Crime-Fraud Exception to the Attorney-Client Privilege", October 2023

provide evidence about Trump's obstruction of justice in refusing to return classified national security documents stored at Mar-a-Lago...public reports suggest that Trump deliberately misled his lawyer. He is said to have lied to Corcoran about the completeness of his search for classified documents at Mar-a-Lago—a lie that Corcoran then dutifully passed along to the government as the truth."[153]

Yet, "[t]he invocation of the crime-fraud exception is remarkable because of the nature of its origins and the deep reluctance with which it is approached by the legal profession. The complexity of the doctrine of crime-fraud...has obscured how genuinely exceptional these events are...we might think that an attorney would be an especially good source of information about a client. But even so, we see a higher value in protecting attorney-client communications against examination."[154]

In other words, the attorney-client privilege is sacrosanct, and the crime-fraud exception is a very rare exception to be employed. If so, one would think it would only be invoked when a client is planning an extraordinarily serious crime; trying to hide his plan to commit a murder for instance or steal an extremely large amount of money by defrauding a bank.

One would not expect such a rare exception to be applied over whether or not an attorney properly certified that some documents were turned over to the Justice Department or not, even if those documents are allegedly classified. This is particularly true when it is unclear whether the former President was hiding documents, and for what purpose - or whether Trump had legal possession of those documents.

As the situation is described by Mark Levin, "Attorney-client privilege is crucial. The crime-fraud exception is a rare exception. It's not supposed to be regularized or routine, or we cease to have the ability to have effective representation of counsel...Mass murderers, terrorists, what have you - attorney-client privilege is rarely pierced when it applies to them, and yet it's been pierced in a serial nature when it applies to Donald Trump...[t]his is just more evidence of the unraveling of our liberties...[o]ur civil liberties are being violated...[i]f

---

[153] Paul Rosenzweig, The Bulwark, "Trump's Attorneys and the Crimes They Enabled", March 31, 2023
[154] Ibid.

they can do this to Donald Trump or if they can drag lawyers in front of grand juries...take their testimony...Well, what's left?"[155]

Unfortunately, this is not the first time Special Counsel Jack Smith has shown a lack of respect for the attorney-client privilege. In 2013, former Arizona Congressman Rick Renzi, a Republican, was convicted of extortion and bribery. "Renzi, who was granted a presidential pardon by Trump, detailed illegal wiretaps, prosecutorial misconduct, and a blatant disregard for the sanctity of attorney-client privilege," by a lawyer working for the man who prosecuted him - Jack Smith.[156]

"Renzi recounted that Smith's team had illegally wiretapped his attorney 41 times. The team not only lied about their activities, but they also tried to utilize the acquired evidence against him. A 2019 legal filing on Renzi's behalf described 'widespread misconduct' and deliberate recording of 'privileged phone calls.' Though the actions were carried out by a member of Smith's prosecutorial team, Smith was responsible for overseeing his team and holding them accountable."[157]

As described in *PJ Media*, "[j]ust as in Renzi's case, the DOJ is allegedly trying to use conversations protected by attorney-client privilege against Donald Trump. Renzi explained that Trump's...attorney-client privilege was infringed on. Smith [claims] that the 'former president was trying to commit a crime by asking' a certain question, even though it was 'normal and proper' attorney-client privileged communication, Renzi stated...Renzi is not the only one to protest against the violation of attorney-client privilege in Trump's case. 'Timothy Parlatore, who until recently worked as a criminal defense attorney for former President Donald Trump,' said Jack Smith's team crossed a 'red line' while Parlatore was testifying before a grand jury...[t]he lawyer's complaint? That questions he was asked infringed on attorney-client privilege."[158]

---

155 Ashley Carnahan, Fox News, "Mark Levin on DOJ's move to pierce Trump's attorney-client privilege: This is the unraveling of our liberties", February 19, 2023

156 Press Release, US Department of Justice, "Former Congressman Richard G. Renzi Sentenced for Extortion and Bribery in Illegal Federal Land Swap", October 28, 2013

157 Anonymous, Deep State Tribunal, "Jack Smith Has Checkered History Of Prosecutorial Misconduct", undated

158 Catherine Salgado, PJ Media, "EXCLUSIVE: Previous Target of DOJ's Trump Legal Hit Squad Details Illegal Wiretaps, 'Misconduct'", June 16, 2023

"Parlatore stated that, in his opinion, it was 'clear that the government was not acting appropriately and made several improper attempts to pierce privilege and, in my opinion, made several significant misstatements to the [grand] jury, which I believe constitutes prosecutorial misconduct.' Not prosecutorial misconduct from the unimpeachable Jack Smith and team! Oh, wait — that's exactly what they were accused of in Renzi's case…"[159]

These are extremely serious allegations of misconduct against Jack Smith and his prosecution team, but the evidence of prior violations of a criminal defendant's right to counsel exist. Could Smith be repeating this illegal pattern in his prosecution of former President Trump?

---

[159]Ibid.

11 THE NEW ALLEGATIONS BROUGHT IN THE FIRST FEDERAL INDICTMENT

In Chapters 2, 3 and 8, we discussed the illegal search of Mar A Lago, and the necessity for the suppression of all evidence seized in the raid as illegally obtained "fruit of the poisonous tree." In Chapter 9, we examined the interaction between the Espionage Act, and the Presidential Records Act, as well as the potential defense that the former President had legal possession of the allegedly classified documents recovered during that illegal search and seizure. Then, in Chapter 10, we reviewed the very serious possibility that Special Counsel Jack Smith and his team have engaged in a pattern of violating the attorney-client privilege rights of the accused, including former President Trump.

In this chapter, we consider the new allegations added to the original Indictment on July 27, 2023, when Special Counsel Jack Smith filed a Superseding Indictment against Trump, his co-defendant and Aide, Waltine Nauta, and now adding Carlos De Oliveira, the Property Manager for Mar A Lago.[160]

The first question many people may have is whether or not the Special Counsel can provide additional allegations and add charges at this stage. The answer is - he sure can. As described by Washington DC lawyers Burnham & Gorokhov, "[t]echnically speaking, an indictment cannot be 'amended' once it has been returned by the grand jury, because that would violate the defendant's Fifth

[160] United States of America v. Donald J. Trump, et al., Superseding Indictment No. 23 CR 80101, United States District Court, Southern District of Florida, July 27, 2023

Amendment right to be indicted by a grand jury. However, it is also true that prosecutors do frequently alter the crimes charged, or even add new charges, during the course of a criminal proceeding. Prosecutors accomplish this by filing what is called a 'superseding' indictment. A superseding indictment is just like any other indictment, and it must be obtained the same way as the original indictment—through a grand jury. The superseding indictment can include different charges, new charges, or add new defendants. Once the grand jury returns a superseding indictment, the superseding indictment replaces (supersedes) the original indictment."[161]

However, as with so many aspects of Special Counsel Jack Smith's investigation and indictment of the former President, a question of legal propriety and fair dealing has arisen regarding the Superseding Indictment. According to *The Washington Post*, "[Florida Federal] Judge Aileen M. Cannon...asked federal prosecutors to explain the use of grand juries in Florida and Washington in the classified documents case against Donald Trump even though charges were filed in South Florida...Cannon...posed the question in a court filing...and told federal prosecutors to respond...'The response shall address the legal propriety of using an out-of-district grand jury proceeding to continue to investigate and/or to seek post-indictment hearings on matters pertinent to the instant indicted matter in this district,' Cannon wrote."[162]

Apparently, "[f]or many months, Justice Department prosecutors had questioned witnesses in the Florida case before a federal grand jury in Washington. The secret proceedings yielded much of the evidence at the crux of the case. But in May, the grand jury activity appeared to continue at a federal courthouse in Miami. Ultimately, prosecutors filed charges in a West Palm Beach courthouse — a courthouse in the same district as Miami and the area where Mar-a-Lago is located...Prosecutors said in a court filing...that they continued to use the grand jury in Washington after they initially charged Trump in June to investigate alleged instances of obstructing the investigation. 'The grand jury in this district and a grand jury in the District of Columbia continued to investigate further obstructive

[161] Anonymous, Burnham & Gorokhov, PLLP, "Federal Indictments: Answers to Frequently Asked Questions", undated

[162] Perry Stein, The Washington Post, "Judge asks prosecutors to justify use of 2 grand juries in Trump documents case", August 8, 2023

activity, and a superseding indictment was returned on July 27, 2023,' prosecutors wrote in the filing."[163]

In other words, "Smith's team used a grand jury in Washington to continue gathering evidence after it had already indicted Trump in Florida using a grand jury in Miami."[164] Is this unusual? Smith is a Special Counsel and has jurisdiction to bring charges against the former President in any jurisdiction in which criminality may have occurred. Thus, he can use more than one Grand Jury in more than one location to investigate charges against Donald Trump.

What is unusual though is the use of a Grand Jury in Washington to continue investigating crimes that allegedly occurred in Florida and are the subject of an indictment brought by another Grand Jury in that state. As described by *Yahoo! News*, "[t]he involvement of multiple grand juries is an issue raised by Trump's lawyers as a potential line of attack against the prosecution because there are rules that limit how and where the government can use them. Cannon's order puts Smith on the spot early on to explain the process."[165]

Turning to the new allegations, it should be noted that the Superseding Indictment corrects a deficiency in the original indictment. As we observed in Chapter 9, Trump was charged with possession of 31 classified documents (out of the 102 allegedly classified documents recovered during the raid on Mar A Lago). The original indictment also described two conversations that Trump had with persons who did not have security clearances, in which he is alleged to have brandished classified documents. One was with a writer, publisher and several members of his staff regarding a "Plan of Attack" prepared for Trump by the Department of Defense; the other with a representative of his political action committee regarding a map related to a military operation. We noted then that "a review of the 31 documents which form the basis for each individual count does not clarify which documents are the basis for the two disclosures described...[n]ot a single one of the documents is described as either a 'Plan' or a 'Map.'"

Perhaps Jack Smith read our original article at usagovpolicy.com, upon which Chapter 9 of this book is based; the July 27 Superseding

[163] Ibid.
[164] Ibid.
[165] Zoe Tillman, Yahoo News, "Trump Documents Case Judge Is Reviewing DOJ Use of Two Grand Juries", August 7, 2023

Indictment has added a 32nd document described as the "Plan of Attack" referenced in the alleged disclosure to the writer and publisher. To date, however, the map described in the second conversation appears to remain unavailable.[166]

Most of the latest allegations involve the new defendant, Carlos De Oliveira. *ABC News* describes the timeline of his involvement as follows; "June 22, 2022 - After observing security footage near the storage room in which classified information was found, the Justice Department sends Trump's lawyers a draft grand jury subpoena for some security footage from cameras near the storage room at Mar-a-Lago...June 23, 2022 - Trump and De Oliveira speak on the phone for 24 minutes...June 24, 2022 - Nauta is told by a coworker that Trump wants to see him. Less than two hours later, Nauta changes his travel schedule to go to Palm Beach, Florida... Nauta and De Oliveira are also in touch that day with each other and an unnamed employee who is identified by Smith's office as the director of information technology at Mar-a-Lago...June 25, 2022 - De Oliveira shares with [an unidentified] Mar-a-Lago employee that Nauta wanted to speak with Mar-a-Lago's director of IT to see 'how long camera footage was stored'...Shortly after arriving in Palm Beach, Florida, that evening, Nauta meets with De Oliveira at Mar-a-Lago, where they go to the security booth where surveillance video is displayed on monitors...June 27, 2022 - De Oliveira walks to the IT office where the director of information technology is working...De Oliveira asks how many days the server retains footage, to which the IT director responds he believes it is 'approximately 45 days'...De Oliveira says 'the boss' wants the server deleted, to which the IT director says said he wouldn't know how to do that and does not believe he has the rights to do that. The IT director tells De Oliveira that De Oliveira would need to reach out to another employee who is supervisor of security for Trump's business organization... De Oliveira [then] texts Nauta...De Oliveira walks through bushes along the northern edge of the Mar-a-Lago property to meet Nauta on the adjacent property....Trump [then] calls De Oliveira and they speak for approximately three and a half minutes."[167]

---

[166] United States of America v. Donald J. Trump, et al., Superseding Indictment No. 23 CR 80101, United States District Court, Southern District of Florida, July 27, 2023

[167] Riley Hoffman and Tal Axelrod, ABC News, "Timeline: How Trump, staffers

Based upon these allegations, Trump, Nauta and De Oliveira are all charged with "Conspiracy to Obstruct Justice," among other charges. The Superseding Indictment alleges the three "did knowingly combine, conspire, confederate, and agree with each other...to engage in misleading conduct toward another person and corruptly persuade another person to withhold a record, document, and other object from an official proceeding," the purpose being "to keep classified documents [Trump] had taken with him from the White House and to hide and conceal them from a federal grand jury."[168]

These activities sound quite nefarious as they are laid out in the Superseding Indictment. But upon examination of the details, the Indictment fails to specify that a criminal conspiracy actually occurred. Instead, the allegations contained in this Indictment lead to a series of questions.

At no time is the substance of any calls between Trump, Nauta and De Oliveira revealed. What did they talk about? While Smith is relying upon the timing of the calls, which would appear to occur just before or after certain actions are taken, there is no indication of how many calls occur between these parties in a given day, and what the conversation between these parties consisted of.

Who is "the boss?" We're supposed to assume it's Trump, but to De Oliveira, Nauta could have been considered his "boss."

De Oliveira asks about deleting Security footage from the camera and is told to speak with the security supervisor. Did De Oliveira then go and speak with that individual? Did Nauta? If not, why not? The Indictment is silent on these issues.

We can answer one additional potential question - was any Security footage deleted? According to the Superseding Indictment, "[i]n July 2022, the FBI and grand jury obtained and reviewed surveillance video from The Mar-a-Lago Club." Trump himself states that "Mar-a-Lago security tapes were not deleted...[t]hey were voluntarily handed over to...Jack Smith. We did not even go to court to stop them from getting these tapes. I never told anybody to delete them."[169]

---

conspired to delete security footage, according to prosecutors", July 27, 2023

[168] United States of America v. Donald J. Trump, et al., Superseding Indictment No. 23 CR 80101, United States District Court, Southern District of Florida, July 27, 2023

Thus, it is clear that no Security footage was ever erased.

Since Trump, Nauta and De Oliveira are charged with Conspiracy, the footage need not have been actually destroyed for the crime to have occurred. It's the agreement between the three of them to attempt to keep evidence from the Grand Jury that would be the crime. "Legally, a Conspiracy exists when 2 or more persons join together and form an agreement to violate the law, and then act on that agreement...only if the government can prove that those involved entered into some agreement to commit the crime and that there was some overt act committed after the agreement was reached to help it succeed. Many times this 'agreement' will be proven by circumstantial evidence. For example, if it can be shown that a participant is receiving some direct benefit from the illegal activity, this is a good indication that the person is a part of the Conspiracy."[170]

It is unclear, at best, what benefit any of these three received from this alleged conspiracy. Further, as noted above, while circumstantial evidence is admissible, unless either Nauta or De Oliveira, or even Trump himself, tells the trial jury whether or not instructions were given to erase the Security footage, that jury can only speculate on what all of these phone calls and meetings have to do with De Oliveira's question to the IT Director.

But more likely than not, the indictment of Nauta and De Oliveira are *intended* to force them to testify against Trump in exchange for a plea deal. Before that happens, however, Special Counsel Smith has to provide the Court with legally sufficient allegations of fact - not a series of events that may or not be connected.

Under Fed. R. Crim. P. 7(c)(1) "The indictment or the information shall be a plain, concise and definite written statement of the essential facts constituting the offense charged."[171] As you read the allegations made against Donald Trump, Waltine Nauta and Carlos De Oliveira in the Superseding Indictment, ask yourself this one crucial question - do you think these allegations sufficiently state a "plain, concise and definite" case of criminal conspiracy?

---

[169] Danielle Wallace, Fox News, "Trump says Mar-a-Lago security tapes 'were not deleted,' accuses special counsel of 'prosecutorial fiction'", July 30, 2023

[170] John Seaman, Federal Law Enforcement Training Centers, "Federal Conspiracy Law (Mp3)", undated

[171] Anonymous, US Department of Justice, Criminal Resource Manual, "221. Sufficiency", undated

While you are thinking about the answer to that question, ask yourself another; Doesn't this prosecution seem like a lot of time and effort to recover 102 documents from someone who has a legitimate argument that he had a legal right to possess those documents?

12 THE BIDEN CRIME FAMILY

This might be a good time to engage in a little "whataboutism," and discuss some of the allegations made about the current President.

If you listen to the legacy media or read the majority of what are generally considered mainstream news sources and you are trying to get information about the Congressional investigation into the Biden Family business, maybe you experience the same feeling as when you come upon a traffic accident, or a crime scene. Usually, there is a police officer waving you away, telling you "Move along citizen, nothing to see here."

Here, it's the media telling you to be on your way and ignore the carnage that's plain to see.

For instance, *Politico* stated in April of 2023 that "House Republicans charged into the majority vowing an investigative onslaught against President Joe Biden and Democrats. But they've gotten almost nowhere so far."[172] Then, in May of 2023, according to *The New York Times*, "[a]fter months of investigation and many public accusations of corruption against Mr. Biden and his family, the first report of the premier House GOP inquiry showed no proof of such misconduct."[173]

These reports are from earlier in the year, before the testimony of Devon Archer to the House Oversight Committee in July. "Archer said...Hunter Biden [made] millions in business deals with...foreign

---

[172] Jordain Carney, Politico, "House GOP's Biden investigations sputter out of the gate", April 4, 2023

[173] Luke Broadwater, The New York Times, "House Republican Report Finds No Evidence of Wrongdoing by President Biden", May 10, 2023

companies, including Burisma and CEFC China Energy," as reported by *Yahoo! News*. "After Burisma added Hunter Biden to its board in 2014, that helped the company survive because it was associated with what Archer called 'the Biden brand...I think Burisma would have gone out of business if it didn't have the brand attached to it,' Archer said. 'People would be intimidated to mess with them.'"[174]

Did this dramatic testimony by Hunter Biden's former business partner change the minds of the media?

No. According to *PBS*, "[t]he Republican-led House Oversight Committee conducted a more than-five hour interview with Devon Archer as part of its expanding congressional inquiry into the Biden family businesses...[b]oth Republican and Democratic lawmakers inside the closed-door interview said Archer testified that over the span of 10 years, Hunter Biden put his father on the phone around 20 times while in the company of associates but 'never once spoke about any business dealings.'"[175]

What did the President talk with his son about during those calls? If you ask New York Democratic Representative Dan Goldman, who was present for Archer's testimony, "The witness was unequivocal and stated very clearly that they never discussed any business on [those] phone conversations...There were niceties. And there was a hello. And [they] talked about the weather or whatever it was...but it was never any business."[176]

The weather? No business discussed? Twenty calls, all while Hunter was "in the company of associates?" Frankly, this doesn't pass the smell test. As the Oversight Committee Republicans asked, "Who dials their father into 20 business phone calls?"[177]

What did Archer actually say? "'You have to understand that there was no business conversation about...a fee or anything like that,' Archer told Congress. 'It was, you know, just general niceties and... conversation in general, you know, about the geography, about the weather, whatever it may be.' Hunter was selling what Archer called

---

[174] John Ward, Yahoo News, "Devon Archer testimony: What Hunter Biden's business partner actually told Congress", August 7, 2023

[175] Farnoush Amiri, PBS, "Hunter Biden sold 'illusion of access' to his father, former business partner tells Congress", July 31, 2023

[176] Ryan King, New York Post, "Rep. Dan Goldman mocked for claim Joe Biden 'talked about the weather' with Hunter's business partners", July 31, 2023

[177] Oversight Committee, X (formerly Twitter), July 31, 2023

an 'illusion of access' to Joe Biden's decision-making power. 'People send signals and those signals are basically used as currency. And that's kind of how a lot of D.C. operators and foreign tycoons and businessmen work,' Archer said."[178]

Besides the 20 phone calls, "Archer also asserted that then-Vice President Joe Biden met a Burisma executive in 2015 at a dinner with Hunter Biden and others in Washington, D.C."[179]

Chairman of the House Oversight Committee, James Comer (R-KY), put the issue in its proper perspective; "Devon Archer's testimony confirms Joe Biden LIED when he said he had no knowledge about his son's business dealings and was not involved. Joe Biden was 'the brand' & he joined Hunter's dinners with his foreign associates in person or by phone over 20 times." (Emphasis in original.)[180]

Indeed. In 2019, candidate Joe Biden stated emphatically that "I have never spoken to my son about his overseas business dealings."[181] Biden also said, "I have never discussed, with my son or my brother or with anyone else, anything having to do with their businesses. Period...And what I will do is the same thing we did in our [Obama] administration. There will be an absolute wall between personal and private [business interests] and the government. There wasn't any hint of scandal at all when we were there. And I'm going to propose the same kind of strict, strict rules. That's why I never talked with my son or my brother or anyone else — even distant family — about their business interests. Period."[182]

These words could be interpreted as being technically true - in those 20 phone calls and even the dinner with a representative from Burisma, the then Vice President did not need to be involved in any discussion of business. As Archer testified, his presence alone, and Hunter's ability to get him on the phone so easily, proved that Hunter had his father's ear.

---

[178] John Ward, Yahoo News, "Devon Archer testimony: What Hunter Biden's business partner actually told Congress", August 7, 2023

[179] Ibid.

[180] Representative James Comer, X (formerly Twitter), July 31, 2023

[181] Justin Baragona, The Daily Beast, "Joe Biden: 'I've Never Spoken to My Son About' Ukraine Business Deals", September 21, 2019

[182] Marc Caputo and Ben Schreckinger, Politico, "Biden pledges 'absolute wall' to separate relatives' business dealings", August 28, 2019

In the words of Lilo Galente, "[a] smart boss finds the sweet spot between being remote enough from street level associates/soldiers who do the dirty work so that he's not easily caught up in law enforcement investigations and being close enough to the hoodlums so that they know that he knows what they're doing or not doing...[t]he boss takes a healthy piece of all of the activities, businesses, or rackets in which the organization is involved. Usually the boss has enough experience to know what most people are doing and how much money they should be earning."[183]

All this comparison between the behavior of Biden and the average crime boss is facetious at best without evidence of actual criminal or unethical activity. So far, the bulk of the hard evidence points toward a pattern of tax evasion and other criminal conduct by the President's son - enough to merit the appointment of a Special Counsel to investigate Hunter Biden's business affairs.[184] What evidence is there of a pattern of criminal and or unethical behavior by the President, and other members of his family?

In May 2023 (as *The New York Times* was claiming that there was "no proof of misconduct"), the House Oversight Committee released a Memorandum detailing some of their findings. "The Committee has subpoenaed four different banks and received thousands of records in response," according to the Memo. "The Committee's bank subpoenas were tailored to specific individuals and companies that engaged in business activities with Biden family members and their business associates."[185]

The Committee reports that "[w]hen President Biden ran as a presidential candidate, he assured the American people his family received no money from China. President Biden recently claimed the Committee's bank records regarding his family's receipt of funds from China are 'not true." Yet, "Biden family members and business associates created a web of over 20 companies—most were limited liability companies formed during Joe Biden's vice presidency...Bank records show the Biden family, their business associates, and their

[183] Lilo Galente, Quora, "What does a mafia boss do exactly? Do they kill and threaten or "just" manage the illegal activities from a safe place?", August 8, 2023

[184] John H. Wilson, usagovpolicy.com, "When is a Special Counsel not a Special Counsel?", August 21, 2023

[185] Memorandum, Committee on Oversight and Accountability Majority Staff to Committee on Oversight and Accountability Majority Members, May 10, 2023

companies received over $10 million from foreign nationals' companies. The Committee has identified payments to Biden family members from foreign companies while Joe Biden served as Vice President and after he left public office...Chinese nationals and companies with significant ties to Chinese intelligence and the Chinese Communist Party hid the source of the funds by layering domestic limited liability companies."[186]

Further, "[t]o date, President Biden has continued to deny that his family received money from China—despite bank records proving otherwise. In 2017 alone, bank records show President Biden's family and their related companies received millions of dollars from Chinese foreign nationals' companies...[b]ecause President Biden is not required to file financial disclosures for immediate family members (other than a spouse or dependents), this gaping legislative hole has allowed President Biden to make misleading statements about the source of his family's income, act willfully blind about their finances notwithstanding potential conflicts of interest, and use federal government resources and personnel—including White House spokespersons—to conceal influence peddling."[187]

The established facts are these; while Joe Biden was Vice President, Hunter Biden engaged in a series of meetings with Chinese, and other foreign nationals. He reportedly "made millions" from these activities. Hunter showed his foreign contacts that he had ready access to his father by calling him during meetings with these overseas associates. The rest of the Biden family then received "millions of dollars" from foreign nationals, including the Chinese, money which was spread between 20 different "shell" companies.

Much of the media will not believe that this "web" of payments does not constitute influence peddling by Joe Biden himself. They would rather view the then Vice President as just an innocent bystander to his son's activities. But the Oversight Committee thinks differently.

"The amount of money involved in these financial transactions is significant. The wires and money transfers range from approximately $5,000 to at least $3 million," the Committee states. "Many of the relevant wire transfers involve Owasco PC, a professional corporation formed in Washington, D.C. Hunter Biden was the

[186] Ibid.

[187] Ibid.

owner of Owasco PC...[t]he transactions in Romania and China show related but separate issues identified by the Committee that raise serious questions about financial disclosures and risks to national security...[t]he Committee is releasing a selection of bank records that shows the Biden family's receipt of money from a foreign company reportedly controlled by Gabriel Popoviciu, the subject of a criminal probe and prosecution for corruption in Romania...[t]hen Vice President Biden delivered speeches and met with Romanian leaders in 2014 and 2015 regarding corruption in the country...[t]he Committee is concerned about the Biden family's pattern of courting business in regions of the world in which the then Vice President had an outsize role and influenced U.S. policy."[188]

Let us take the position that these are mere allegations. But are these allegations, involving the current President of the United States, serious enough to require a full investigation, and the appointment of a Special Counsel?

If you ask Attorney General Merrick Garland, he has already appointed a Special Counsel, and his name is David Weiss. "Mr. Weiss, in his capacity as U.S. Attorney and along with federal law enforcement partners, began investigating allegations of certain criminal conduct by, *among others*, Robert Hunter Biden," Garland stated when he appointed Weiss as Special Counsel on August 11, 2023 (Emphasis added). "As Special Counsel, he will continue to have the authority and responsibility that he has previously exercised to oversee the investigation and decide where, when, and whether to file charges."[189]

It is argued that the "among others" referenced above includes the President himself. but significantly, nowhere is it stated that David Weiss is involved in any investigation beyond that of Hunter Biden's activities.

In fact, as reported by *Newsweek*, "[t]he GOP-led House Oversight Committee wrote on X that Garland's move is part of a cover up aimed to discredit the 'Committee's mounting evidence of President Joe Biden's role in his family's schemes selling 'the brand' for millions of dollars to foreign nationals.'"[190]

---

[188] Ibid.

[189] Speech, US Department of Justice, "Attorney General Merrick B. Garland Delivers a Statement", August 11, 2023

[190] Nick Mordowanec, Newsweek, "David Weiss' Appointment as Hunter Biden

Is this assertion true? Judge for yourself. As we stated in August of 2023, in a column for usagovpolicy.com, "rather than select someone from outside the Justice Department, Attorney General Merrick Garland chose the current US Attorney for Delaware, David Weiss, to serve as his Special Counsel – the same David Weiss who has conducted an investigation into Hunter Biden for five years, failed to bring felony charges against Hunter Biden in a timely manner, failed to bring a routine felony gun charge against the President's son, offered Hunter a plea to two misdemeanors and a diversion program, and then watched that agreement blow up under questioning by a federal judge."[191]

It is therefore safe to conclude that even if David Weiss is conducting an investigation of Joe Biden and the rest of his family for the unethical and potentially criminal activities outlined by the House Oversight Committee, we can expect the same incompetent and "slow walked" investigation we have witnessed Weiss conduct regarding the President's son.

Let us be honest here - given the evidence uncovered by the House Oversight Committee, the American people deserve better than David Weiss to look into these serious allegations.

Special Counsel Raises Questions", August 11, 2023

[191] John H. Wilson, usagovpolicy.com, "When is a Special Counsel not a Special Counsel?", August 21, 2023

13 THE SECOND FEDERAL INDICTMENT

In our Introduction, we briefly discussed the Second Impeachment of former President Donald Trump. For those who do not remember, or who have just emerged from a coma, shortly after the January 6, 2021 riot at the Capitol, Democratic members of the House of Representatives voted an Article of Impeachment against Trump for one count of Incitement of Insurrection. Specifically, "by inciting violence against the Government of the United States...President Trump repeatedly issued false statements asserting that the Presidential election results were the product of widespread fraud and should not be accepted by the American people or certified by State or Federal officials."[192]

"On January 6, 2021," the Article of Impeachment states, "pursuant to the 12th Amendment to the Constitution of the United States, the Vice President of the United States, the House of Representatives, and the Senate met at the United States Capitol for a Joint Session of Congress to count the votes of the Electoral College. In the months preceding the Joint Session, President Trump repeatedly issued false statements asserting that the Presidential election results were the product of widespread fraud and should not be accepted by the American people or certified by State or Federal officials."[193]

The Article of Impeachment continued; "Trump, addressed a crowd at the Ellipse in Washington, DC (on January 6). There, he reiterated false claims that 'we won this election, and we won it by a

[192] House Resolution No. 24, January 25, 2021

[193] Ibid.

landslide.' He also willfully made statements that, in context, encouraged—and foreseeably resulted in—lawless action at the Capitol, such as: 'if you don't fight like hell you're not going to have a country anymore.' Thus incited by President Trump, members of the crowd he had addressed, in an attempt to, among other objectives, interfere with the Joint Session's solemn constitutional duty to certify the results of the 2020 Presidential election, unlawfully breached and vandalized the Capitol, injured and killed law enforcement personnel, menaced Members of Congress, the Vice President, and Congressional personnel, and engaged in other violent, deadly, destructive, and seditious acts."[194]

Of course, this impeachment did not accurately summarize Trump's comments on January 6. In fact, these are Trump's actual words from his speech at the Ellipse that day; "Our country has had enough. We will not take it anymore and that's what this is all about. To use a favorite term that all of you people really came up with, we will stop the steal... Now it is up to Congress to confront this egregious assault on our democracy. After this, we're going to walk down and I'll be there with you...We're going to walk down to the Capitol, and we're going to cheer on our brave senators, and congressmen and women...You have to show strength, and you have to be strong."[195]

"These words occurred towards the beginning of his speech. Near the end, as we noted in the Introduction, President Trump said '[w]e're going to walk down Pennsylvania Avenue, I love Pennsylvania Avenue, and we're going to the Capitol and we're going to try and give...our Republicans, the weak ones, because the strong ones don't need any of our help, we're going to try and give them the kind of pride and boldness that they need to take back our country.'"[196]

Besides the inaccurate and misleading use of Trump's words, the Impeachment contained various other misstatements of fact. For instance, while law enforcement personnel were injured, none were killed on January 6. In fact, the only person killed that day was an unarmed protestor, Ashli Babbitt, who was shot to death by Capitol Police Lieutenant Michael Byrd. (An internal investigation cleared the

---

[194] Ibid.
[195] Brian Naylor NPR, "Read Trump's Jan. 6 Speech, A Key Part Of Impeachment Trial", February 10, 2021
[196] Ibid.

officer of wrongdoing.)[197]

Trump did call the 2020 election results into question and did call on "Vice President Pence to reject Biden's win and send the results back to the states... [h]owever, Pence said it is 'my considered judgment that my oath to support and defend the Constitution constrains me from claiming unilateral authority to determine which electoral votes should be counted and which should not.'"[198]

The riot at the Capitol followed Trump's speech, and VP Pence's refusal to agree to the former President's wishes.

Predictably, this Impeachment ended in the same fashion as the first - with an acquittal of President Trump by the Senate - and that had *NPR* worried. "The verdict closes the book on this Trump presidency, though the Senate, by not convicting and barring him from holding public office in the future, left open the possibility that Trump, a 74-year-old Republican, could run again for president."[199]

Sure enough, just as *NPR* feared, Donald Trump announced his campaign to run for President of the United States in the 2024 election. "'In order to make America great and glorious again, I am tonight announcing my candidacy for president of the United States,' Trump told a crowd (in November of 2022) at Mar-a-Lago, his waterfront estate in Florida, where his campaign will be headquartered."[200]

As we discussed in Chapter 2, in August of 2022, before Trump had even announced his candidacy, the FBI conducted a search of the former President's home in South Florida in an effort to recover documents Trump was allegedly withholding from the National Archives. We have argued that this search was illegal, based upon an unconstitutionally overbroad search warrant. Then, subsequent to Trump's announcement of his campaign, as we discussed in Chapters 4 through 6, in the Spring of 2023, Trump was indicted by the New York County District Attorney, Alvin Bragg, for allegedly falsifying

---

[197] Geoffrey Alpert, Jef Noble, and Seth Stoughton, Law Fare, "Evaluating the Police Shooting of Ashli Babbitt", September 9, 2021

[198] Brian Naylor NPR, "Trump Calls on Pence To Reject Electoral Votes. Pence Says He Won't", January 6, 2021

[199] Domenico Montanaro, NPR, "Senate Acquits Trump In Impeachment Trial - Again", February 13, 2021

[200] Gabby Orr, Kristen Holmes, and Veronica Stracqualursi, CNN, "Former President Donald Trump announces a White House bid for 2024", November 16, 2022

business records in an effort to conceal payments made from his 2016 campaign to porno actress Stormy Daniels.

Once that line had been crossed, and a former President of the United States was indicted for criminal charges, in June of 2023, Special Counsel Jack Smith brought an indictment against Trump in a Florida Federal Court, alleging that the former President violated the Espionage Act by being in possession of classified documents, evidence which was obtained in the August 2022 search of Mar A Lago. (See, Chapters 7 through 10.)

Not satisfied with his Florida indictment of Trump, Smith then used a Grand Jury in Washington DC to revisit the subject of the second Trump impeachment - the former President's actions on January 6, 2023. The result? Yet another federal indictment of Donald J. Trump.

According to this Indictment, filed with the DC District Court on August 1, 2023, "The Defendant lost the 2020 presidential election...[d]espite having lost, the Defendant was determined to remain in power. So, for more than two months following election day on November 3, 2020, the Defendant spread lies that there had been outcome-determinative fraud in the election and that he had actually won. These claims were false, and the Defendant knew that they were false. But the Defendant repeated and widely disseminated them anyway—to make his knowingly false claims appear legitimate, create an intense national atmosphere of mistrust and anger, and erode public faith in the administration of the election."[201]

We know that Jack Smith favors what are called "talking indictments" - that is, the prosecutor provides a narrative of the criminal acts he alleges form the basis for the criminal charges. But this Indictment reads more like an Op-Ed piece in *The New York Times* than a legal document.

When we reach the heart of the charges, there are three separate conspiracies the former President is alleged to have engaged in:

"a) A conspiracy to defraud the United States by using dishonesty, fraud, and deceit to impair, obstruct, and defeat the lawful federal government function by which the results of the presidential election are collected, counted, and certified by the federal government, in violation of 18 USC Sec. 371; b) A conspiracy to corruptly obstruct

[201] United States of America v. Donald J. Trump, Indictment No. 23 CR 257, United States District Court, District of Columbia, August 1, 2023

and impede the January 6 congressional proceeding at which the collected results of the presidential election are counted and certified ("the certification proceeding"), in violation of 18 USC Sec. 1512(k); and c) A conspiracy against the right to vote and to have one's vote counted, in violation of 18 USC Sec. 241."[202]

To achieve these goals, Trump and his un-named and un-indicted co-conspirators are alleged to have "attempted to enlist the Vice President to use his ceremonial role at the January 6 certification proceeding to fraudulently alter the election results...using knowingly false claims of election fraud, the Defendant and co-conspirators attempted to convince the Vice President to...reject legitimate electoral votes...[w]hen that failed, on the morning of January 6, the Defendant and co-conspirators repeated knowingly false claims of election fraud to gathered supporters, falsely told them that the Vice President had the authority to and might alter the election results, and directed them to the Capitol to obstruct the certification proceeding and exert pressure on the Vice President to take the fraudulent actions he had previously refused."[203]

The Indictment further states that "[a]fter it became public on the afternoon of January 6 that the Vice President would not fraudulently alter the election results, a large and angry crowd— including many individuals whom the Defendant had deceived into believing the Vice President could and might change the election results— violently attacked the Capitol and halted the proceeding. As violence ensued, the Defendant and co-conspirators exploited the disruption by redoubling efforts to levy false claims of election fraud and convince Members of Congress to further delay the certification based on those claims."[204]

Compare these allegations to those made almost two years previously in the Second Trump Impeachment. Aren't the allegations brought in the Second Trump federal indictment basically the same as those for which he was impeached?

Under the Fifth Amendment to the US Constitution, "[n]o person shall be...subject for the same offence to be twice put in jeopardy of life or limb." This "prohibition against 'double jeopardy' was designed to protect an individual from being subjected to the hazards

---

[202] Ibid.

[203] Ibid.

[204] Ibid.

of trial and possible conviction more than once for an alleged offense. . . .The underlying idea, one that is deeply ingrained in at least the Anglo-American system of jurisprudence, is that the State with all its resources and power should not be allowed to make repeated attempts to convict an individual for an alleged offense, thereby subjecting him to embarrassment, expense and ordeal and compelling him to live in a continuing state of anxiety and insecurity, as well as enhancing the possibility that even though innocent he may be found guilty."[205]

The law of double jeopardy is not absolute. As OJ Simpson discovered, "if a defendant is tried for a criminal case, double jeopardy does not protect them from also being tried for a related offense in civil court. For instance, if the state brings murder charges against a defendant, the family of the victim may also sue the defendant for punitive damages."[206] But pertinent to our analysis, "Double jeopardy does not prevent multiple charges for the same crime from different jurisdictions. If a crime violated the laws of multiple states, then each state may press charges. Likewise, if a crime violated both state and federal law, then it would be allowable to have two criminal suits for the same crime."[207]

If the allegations contained in the second federal indictment are substantially the same as those brought in the second impeachment, how can Trump be prosecuted in federal court for actions for which he was acquitted by Congress?

At first blush, it would appear that there is no prohibition to bringing criminal charges against Donald Trump after his second impeachment failed. "The Senate's impeachment trial was not a judicial proceeding; the parties are not the same; and...the Senate's judgment does not have legal effect."[208]

In fact, according to a Justice Department memorandum from 2000, "[t]he Constitution permits a former President to be indicted and tried for the same offenses for which he was impeached by the House of Representatives and acquitted by the Senate."[209] Their

---

[205] Anonymous, Justia, "Double Jeopardy" with Annotations, undated

[206] Daniel Goldberg, goldbergdefense.com, "Understanding double jeopardy and its exceptions", February 23, 2018

[207] Ibid.

[208] Steve Vladeck, MSNBC, "How Trump weaponized his impeachment acquittal", May 26, 2021

reasoning?

"[i]mpeachment and trial by the Senate, on the one hand, and prosecution in the courts, on the other, 'serve different ends...those different ends...seem to be protection of our institutions of government from corrupt or incompetent officials...impeachment trials 'may sometimes be influenced by political passions and interests that would be rigorously excluded from a criminal trial.'"[210]

Further, "if the scope of the Impeachment...were restricted to convicted parties, 'the failure of the House to vote an impeachment, or the failure of the impeachment in the Senate, would confer upon the civil officer accused complete and - were the statute of limitations permitted to run - permanent immunity from criminal prosecution however plain his guilt'...such a view would give Congress an indirect power of pardon - via impeachment and acquittal - even though the Constitution vests the President alone with the power to pardon."[211]

The DOJ memorandum references the Impeachment Judgment Clause (Article 1, Section 3, Clause 7 of the US Constitution), which states that "Judgment in Cases of Impeachment shall not extend further than to removal from Office, and disqualification to hold and enjoy any Office of honor, Trust, or Profit under the United States: but the Party convicted shall nevertheless be liable and subject to Indictment, Trial, Judgment, and Punishment, according to Law." The Justice Department admits that this "clause is ambiguous when it comes to officials who have been impeached and not convicted...[the] failure to mention parties acquitted by the Senate implies that they, unlike convicted parties, are not subject to regular criminal prosecution."[212]

Nonetheless, DOJ concluded that "the Impeachment Judgment Clause was intended to make sure both that the special legislative court (the Senate) for the largely political offenses justifying impeachment would be able to impose only political, not ordinary criminal punishments and that offenders who also violated regular criminal laws would not stand above the law because they had been

---

209 Memorandum Opinion, US Attorney General, "Whether a Former President May Be Indicted and Tried for the Same Offenses for Which He was Impeached by the House and Acquitted by the Senate", August 18, 2000

210 Ibid.

211 Ibid.

212 Ibid.

officeholders when they committed their misdeeds...James Wilson, a leading figure at the Constitutional Convention... argued, 'Though they may not be convicted on impeachment before the Senate, they may be tried by their country; and if their criminality is established, the law will punish.'"[213]

In other words, since there are different purposes and penalties, an impeachment does not provide the protections of double jeopardy, whether the impeached federal official is convicted or acquitted - even though the Impeachment Judgment Clause only mentions criminal punishment for *convicted* federal officials.

At least, that's the position of the Justice Department. *Breitbart* Editor Joel Pollak has another view.

"The Double Jeopardy Clause, contained within the Fifth Amendment, prevents any person from being tried twice in a federal court for the same crime." Pollak states. "It does not prevent someone from being tried for the same crime in a state court and a federal court, because state and federal governments are considered to be 'dual sovereigns.' But it applies to the federal level — and while an impeachment trial in the Senate is not a formal criminal proceeding, it has many of the same features as a federal criminal trial... the Constitution's Impeachment Clause...does *not* say that a person who has been *acquitted* by the Senate can still be subject to the criminal process." (Emphasis in original.)[214]

Thus, Pollak reasons, "[a]rguably, the Constitution intended to protect an acquitted official. That seems even more convincing when considering that the standard of proof in the Senate is *lower* than in a criminal court — there is no requirement of proof beyond a reasonable doubt. As Alexander Hamilton himself observed in Federalist 65, a Senate trial risks of being decided by political factors. An acquittal there is *harder* to win than one in court. Therefore, Trump is protected by the Double Jeopardy Clause. The new indictment should be quashed before trial, and the country should be spared the drama." (Emphasis in original.)[215]

Further support for the application of Double Jeopardy is given by Rodin, writing on the website *Ricochet*; "the key question is

---

213 Ibid.

214 Joel B. Pollak, Breitbart, "Trump Cannot Be Tried for January 6 Under Double Jeopardy Clause", August 2, 2023

215 Ibid.

whether the Senate trial constituted a court proceeding. And here, the decision of Chief Justice Roberts to not preside in the second impeachment trial may be critical. It is hard to imagine that a proceeding conducted under the chief judicial officer is not a 'trial' for purposes of double jeopardy. But Roberts did not preside, and at the time, his decision not to do so (as no current officer holder was on trial) raised interesting questions about its legitimacy. But the officer who did preside, Senator Pat Leahy of Vermont, assured us - 'When I preside over the impeachment trial of former President Donald Trump, I will not waver from my constitutional and sworn obligations to administer the trial with fairness, in accordance with the Constitution and the laws.' So, Senator Leahy certainly thought it was a trial."[216]

Unfortunately, the view of Senator Pat Leahy does not control this issue; it will be the opinion of the federal judge presiding over the Second Trump indictment that will be determinative.

That is until the inevitable appeal of the judge's ruling, no matter which way she rules.

---

[216] Rodin, Ricochet, "Is the Trump Indictment Barred as Double Jeopardy?", Augugst 3, 2023

14 JACK SMITH AND THE THOUGHT POLICE

There was a time when it was safe to assume that we had all read George Orwell's novel, *1984.* But that time has passed, and there are many readers who have undoubtedly heard references to this seminal work, without having actually read the book. Therefore, a brief refresher course on one of the principle concepts from this novel is necessary - the theory of thoughtcrime.

"Even if someone leaves these thoughts unspoken, it is still a crime to think them. It is one of the scariest parts of Winston Smith's world in *1984.* The person who thinks these thoughts is held responsible for them as though they said them out loud or committed the act they were thinking about...To understand thoughtcrime, it's important to understand the consequences of committing it. If one were to have illegal thoughts and those thoughts showed on their face, or they expressed them in some way, they're going to be arrested by the Thought Police. This group is responsible for hunting down thought criminals and bringing them to the Ministry of Love. This aptly named ministry reforms and kills thought criminals."[217]

With this description of "thoughtcrime" in mind, let us review some of the allegations made in Special Counsel Jack Smith's August 2023 federal indictment of former President Donald Trump: "[f]or more than two months following election day on November 3, 2020, the Defendant spread lies that there had been outcome-determinative fraud in the election and that he had actually won. These claims were false, and the Defendant knew that they were false... The

[217] Emma Baldwin, Book Analysis, "Thoughtcrime," undated

Defendant...made knowingly false claims that there had been outcome-determinative fraud in the 2020 presidential election...These claims were false, and the Defendant knew that they were false."[218]

How is it that Jack Smith knows what Donald Trump was thinking? According to the Indictment, "the Defendant was notified repeatedly that his claims were untrue—often by the people on whom he relied for candid advice on important matters, and who were best positioned to know the facts— and he deliberately disregarded the truth."[219]

In other words, Donald Trump knew that there wasn't any "outcome determinative fraud" in the 2020 presidential election because other people told him so.

And who were these people that told Donald Trump there was no evidence of "outcome determinative" election fraud in the 2020 presidential election? According to Smith, these people included "Vice President [Mike Pence]...[who]...told the Defendant that he had seen no evidence of outcome-determinative fraud." There were also "[t]he senior leaders of the Justice Department...[who]...told the Defendant on multiple occasions that various allegations of fraud were unsupported;" "Senior White House attorneys ... [who] ... informed the Defendant that there was no evidence of outcome-determinative election fraud," and "State and federal courts ... [who] ... rejected every outcome-determinative post-election lawsuit filed by the Defendant, his coconspirators, and allies, providing the Defendant real-time notice that his allegations were meritless."[220]

As a result of Donald Trump's refusal to accept that he had actually lost the 2020 presidential election, and based upon the former President's "false" belief that election fraud was pervasive in that election, according to the indictment, "The Defendant's knowingly false statements were integral to his criminal plans to defeat the federal government function, obstruct the certification, and interfere with others' right to vote and have their votes counted."[221]

These allegations regarding what Trump chose to believe would seem to fit the very definition of a thought crime. From all

---

[218] United States of America v. Donald J. Trump, Indictment No. 23 CR 257, United States District Court, District of Columbia, August 1, 2023

[219] Ibid.

[220] Ibid.

[221] Ibid.

appearances, Trump believed there was election fraud, that it was indeed "outcome determinative," and as a result, he challenged the results of the election in every way possible.

In a criminal case, the prosecution must establish that a defendant has *mens rea* - that is, criminal intent. "The literal translation from Latin is '*guilty mind*'...[e]stablishing the *mens rea* of an offender, in addition to the *actus reus* (physical elements of the crime) is usually necessary to prove guilt in a criminal trial. The prosecution typically must prove beyond reasonable doubt that the defendant committed the offense with a culpable state of mind." As stated by the US Supreme Court in *Staples v. United States*, "[t]he *mens rea* requirement is premised upon the idea that one must possess a guilty state of mind and be aware of his or her misconduct."[222]

Even if Trump's belief in election fraud was mistaken (an open question, as we shall discuss), to all appearances, his belief was an honest one. In an interview in September of 2023 with *Meet the Press*, Trump maintained his view that he actually won the 2020 presidential election. "The former president said he didn't listen to his attorneys who told him he had lost the election because he didn't respect them and that he 'respected many others that said the election was rigged...I was listening to different people, and when I added it all up, the election was rigged,' Trump told NBC's Kristen Welker. He added, 'You know who I listen to? Myself. I saw what happened.'"[223]

But an inability to establish what was in the mind of Donald Trump doesn't stop Jack Smith - Trump's belief was not mistaken, it was false! Why? Because people in the Justice Department, some lawyers and some courts told him so!

In effect, Smith's indictment seeks to establish Trump's *mens rea* through his *actus reus* - that is, his allegedly guilty mind is reflected by his allegedly guilty actions. Proceeding from the premise that Trump couldn't possibly believe that he'd been robbed of the Presidency, Smith outlines a series of actions taken by the former President "in his criminal efforts to overturn the legitimate results of the 2020 presidential election and retain power."[224]

---

[222] Cornell Law School, Legal Information Institute, "mens rea", undated

[223] Kate Sullivan, CNN, "Trump acknowledges he was told 2020 election lies were false in wide-ranging interview", September 18, 2023

[224] United States of America v. Donald J. Trump, Indictment No. 23 CR 257,

For instance, Trump "said that there had been a suspicious vote dump in Detroit, Michigan... stating, 'In Detroit, there were hours of unexplained delay in delivering many of the votes for counting. The final batch did not arrive until four in the morning and—even though the polls closed at eight o'clock. So they brought it in, and the batches came in, and nobody knew where they came from.'"[225]

According to Smith, "[o]n December 1, [2020] the Defendant raised his Michigan vote dump claim with the Attorney General, who responded that what had occurred in Michigan had been the normal vote counting process and that there was no indication of fraud in Detroit...[d]espite this, the next day, the Defendant made a knowingly false statement that in Michigan, '[a]t 6:31 in the morning, a vote dump of 149,772 votes came in unexpectedly. We were winning by a lot. That batch was received in horror. Nobody knows anything about it. It's corrupt. Detroit is corrupt. I have a lot of friends in Detroit. They know it. But Detroit is totally corrupt.'"[226]

Was this a "knowingly false" statement? Or can it be demonstrated that Donald Trump had a basis to believe that the Attorney General was wrong, and there was a "suspicious vote dump" in Detroit, Michigan?

According to the *Gateway Pundit*, "a wide variety of eyewitnesses...observed fraud just in Michigan. Many of those observers mentioned a very suspicious 3:30AM Biden Ballot Dump of votes in Detroit at the TCF Center where absentees were being counted...Detroit elections worker whistleblower Jessy Jacob testified... that there were no ballots left to process at the Detroit Department of Elections by 8:30PM on election night... Every single witness the Gateway Pundit has spoken with said that there were no ballots left to count and tabulate by around 9:00PM on election night at the TCF Center. Many left the location because there was nothing left to do..."[227]

Then, security camera footage shows a "white van clearly delivering ballots (at about 3:30 AM)", an event confirmed by "City

---

United States District Court, District of Columbia, August 1, 2023

[225] Ibid.

[226] Ibid.

[227] Benjamin Wetmore, The Gateway Pundit, "2000 Mules Just "Tip of the Voter Fraud Iceberg" – Michigan Investigators Reveal Mountain of New Evidence of 2020 Election Fraud", May 16, 2022

of Detroit Senior Advisor to the City Clerk Chris Thomas." However, Thomas "claims that only 16,000 ballots arrived in the 3:30AM Biden Ballot Dump."[228]

Thomas' information is partially supported by The Edison data from Michigan, which "show[s] voter results in real-time, a service offered to media outlets." However, "the Edison data for Michigan shows a major spike of late ballots in Wayne County/Detroit...Michigan added 149,000 votes for Biden at 6:31am the day after the election, where 94% of the votes were for Joe Biden. Where did those votes come from if most of the other counties had already reported their final totals by 8:00PM on election night?"[229]

A good question. Here is how *The Associated Press* answers; "The 8 p.m. deadline on Election Day in Michigan was for voters to cast their ballots, not for those ballots to be delivered or counted. In big cities such as Detroit, it can take several hours for ballots to go through security checks before being sent to counting locations. That process is customary and legal, according to Michigan Secretary of State Jocelyn Benson's office...[t]he conservative website The Gateway Pundit is using a new video to recycle old misinformation about Michigan's presidential election on Nov. 3...[b]ut this article and video don't show proof of fraud. These false claims are based on a misunderstanding of the ballot deadline and how ballot deliveries work in large jurisdictions such as Detroit."[230]

The AP admits that "[i]t's true that a white van used by the city arrived at the TCF Center to deliver ballots in the early hours of the morning on Nov. 4, according to a sworn affidavit from Christopher Thomas, a former state elections chief who worked at the TCF Center on election night," but asserts that "there was nothing fraudulent or illegal about that. 'Early in the morning on Wednesday, November 4, approximately 16,000 ballots were delivered in a white van used by the city,' Thomas said in his affidavit. 'The ballots delivered to the TCF Center had been verified by the City Clerk's staff prior to delivery in a process prescribed by Michigan law.'"[231]

Sure enough, "[i]n a Nov. 13 order, Wayne County Circuit Chief

---

[228] Ibid.

[229] Ibid

[230] Ali Swenson, AP News, "Video taken election night doesn't show illegal activity in Detroit", February 8, 2021

[231] Ibid.

Judge Timothy Kenny declined to stop the certification of Detroit-area votes, ruling that allegations of fraud at the TCF Center on election night were 'incorrect and not credible.'"[232]

It sounds reasonable that the deadline for votes to be registered at the poll is 8 PM. It also sounds reasonable that it might take some time for those ballots to travel from the polling place to the counting location. But this location was the TCF Center - where ABSENTEE ballots were being processed, not ballots cast on Election Day. What explains a delay of more than 7 hours (from 8 PM to 3:30 AM) to transfer 16,000 Absentee ballots to the TCF Center - ballots that should have already been at the Center, ready to count once the polls had closed?

Further, what about the Edison data which shows 149,000 additional votes for Biden by 6:31 AM? If there were only 16,000 votes on that 3:30 AM van, where did the other 133,000 votes for Biden come from? The *AP* doesn't say. Instead, they assure the reader that their article "is part of *The Associated Press*' ongoing effort to fact-check misinformation that is shared widely online, including work with Facebook to identify and reduce the circulation of false stories on the platform."[233]

Think back to the statement Trump gave that Jack Smith alleges to be "knowingly false." "At 6:31 in the morning, a vote dump of 149,772 votes came in unexpectedly" the former President stated. As we have discussed, by 6:31 AM there is evidence that "Michigan added 149,000 votes for Biden at 6:31am the day after the election." Trump calls this a "vote dump," and then goes on to say, "Detroit is totally corrupt."[234]

Other than Trump's claim that "we were winning by a lot" (which is highly unlikely in the Democratic stronghold of Detroit, Michigan), where is the "knowing falsehood" in the former President's statements? Where does the President evidence anything but a sincere belief that those votes came in late, after the polls had closed, and that this was a corrupt action?

Even if its circumstantial at best, isn't there some evidence that 16,000 absentee ballots taking 7 hours to reach a counting location,

---

[232] Ibid.

[233] Ibid.

[234] United States of America v. Donald J. Trump, Indictment No. 23 CR 257, United States District Court, District of Columbia, August 1, 2023

and another 133,000 votes showing up by 6:30 in the morning, is unusual, and could lead one to believe that fraudulent activity had occurred?

Under Jack Smith's theory of his case, is Donald Trump required to believe his Attorney General when he states, "that there was no indication of fraud in Detroit?" Or is Trump entitled to his own opinion, based on the facts discussed above?

In fact, Trump is not alone is this opinion. According to *NBC*, in June of 2023, "A new Monmouth poll finds 30% of respondents believe Biden's victory came thanks to voter fraud...[t]hat share is virtually unchanged in Monmouth's polling since November of 2020 - the share of Americans who believe it remained between 32% and 29%... Virtually all Democrats (93%) say Biden won the election fairly, a view shared by 58% of independents. Just 21% of Republicans believe Biden won his election fair and square, while 68% say he won 'due to voter fraud.' That's very similar to Monmouth's findings in the weeks after the 2020 election, when 18% of Republicans, 67% of independents and 95% of Democrats said Biden's election victory was fair."[235]

Of course, *NBC* is appalled by this result, saying it "highlights the disconnect on one of the foundational issues facing American democracy... [t]here remains no evidence that widespread fraud substantially affected the outcome of the 2020 election."[236]

So then why do people persist in believing that the election was stolen from Trump? Why does Trump?

Maybe because there is some evidence to support this belief, despite the efforts by much of the press to put this story to rest. Maybe, under the First Amendment to the US Constitution, we also have a right to believe what we want to believe - and Donald Trump is included with those holding that right.

On its face, then, Jack Smith's attempt to prosecute Donald Trump for the thoughtcrime of not believing the "experts" and his lawyers is a threat to the rights of the rest of us to believe what we wish - even if it turns out to be wrong or mistaken - and especially if we know in our hearts that its true.

---

[235] Ben Kamisar, NBC News, "Almost a third of Americans still believe the 2020 election result was fraudulent", June 20, 2023

[236] Ibid.

15 IS IT ILLEGAL TO SEEK THE APPOINTMENT OF ALTERNATE ELECTORS?

In Chapter 13, we discussed whether or not Double Jeopardy would apply to the Second federal indictment of former President Trump, given that the Senate already acquitted the 45th President for substantially similar charges. In Chapter 14, we discussed the impossibility of establishing that Donald Trump had a "guilty mind" when he asserted that he had not lost the 2020 Presidential Election.

In this chapter we review an allegation made in the second federal indictment that may be just as hard to prove as whether or not Donald Trump truly believed he was fraudulently deprived of his office; The use of alternative electors.

Under Article II of the Constitution of the United States, the method for choosing the President and Vice-President of the United States is described in detail; "Each State shall appoint, in such Manner as the Legislature thereof may direct, a Number of Electors," Section 1 states. "The Electors shall meet in their respective States, and vote by Ballot for two Persons...they shall make a List of all the Persons voted for, and of the Number of Votes for each, which List they shall sign and certify, and transmit sealed to the Seat of the Government of the United States, directed to the President of the Senate. The President of the Senate shall, in the Presence of the Senate and House of Representatives, open all the Certificates, and the Votes shall then be counted. The Person having the greatest Number of Votes shall be the President."[237]

---

[237] Michael Ramsey and Stephen Vladeck, National Constitution Center, "Commander in Chief Clause Common Interpretation", undated

The original Article II called for the Electors to vote for two people, with the intention that the one with the most votes would become President, and the second-place finisher Vice-President. However, as described by the National Constitution Center, "The most glaring early bugs in the system—the real possibility of ties [and] the fact that the president and vice-president could represent different political parties as had happened when Adams and Jefferson served together in 1796—were ironed out by the Twelfth Amendment in 1804."[238]

Under the Twelfth Amendment, "The Electors...shall name in their ballots the person voted for as President, and in distinct ballots the person voted for as Vice-President, and they shall make distinct lists of all persons voted for as President, and of all persons voted for as Vice-President, and of the number of votes for each." There then follows a complicated series of rules for resolving tied votes, including directing that "if no person have such majority, then from the persons having the highest numbers not exceeding three on the list of those voted for as President, the House of Representatives shall choose immediately, by ballot, the President."

This "Electoral College" is described by Darrell West in an article for the Brookings Institute; "The framers of the Constitution set up the Electoral College for a number of different reasons. According to Alexander Hamilton in Federalist Paper Number 68, the body was a compromise at the Constitutional Convention in Philadelphia between large and small states. Many of the latter worried that states such as Massachusetts, New York, Pennsylvania, and Virginia would dominate the presidency, so they devised an institution where each state had Electoral College votes in proportion to the number of its senators and House members. The former advantaged small states since each state had two senators regardless of its size, while the latter aided large states because the number of House members was based on the state's population."[239]

While West himself believes that the Electoral College has outlived its usefulness and should be abolished, he admits that "there are clear partisan divisions in these sentiments. In 2000, while the presidential election outcome was still being litigated, a Gallup survey

---

[238] Ibid.

[239] Darrell M. West, Brookings, "It's Time to Abolish the Electoral College", October 15, 2019

reported that 73 percent of Democratic respondents supported a constitutional amendment to abolish the Electoral College and move to direct popular voting, but only 46 percent of Republican respondents supported that view. This gap has since widened as after the 2016 election, 81 percent of Democrats and 19 percent of Republicans affirmatively answered the same question."[240]

According to Special Counsel Jack Smith's "January 6th" indictment, Donald Trump "pursued unlawful means of discounting legitimate votes and subverting the election results." He allegedly did so by organizing "fraudulent slates of electors in seven targeted states (Arizona, Georgia, Michigan, Nevada, New Mexico, Pennsylvania, and Wisconsin), [and] attempting to mimic the procedures that the legitimate electors were supposed to follow under the Constitution and other federal and state laws. This included causing the fraudulent electors to meet on the day appointed by federal law on which legitimate electors were to gather and cast their votes; cast fraudulent votes for the Defendant; and sign certificates falsely representing that they were legitimate electors."[241]

While Smith uses the word "fraudulent" to describe the gathering of these alternate electors, the heart of these allegations lead to a fundamental question - is it illegal to organize alternate electors?

According to Constitutional Law Professor Ed Foley, "[a] key component of the effort to negate Joe Biden's Electoral College victory...was the submission for congressional consideration of purported electoral votes cast for Trump from seven battleground states...Joe Biden won the popular vote in all these states...[t]he actual electors appointed in these states pursuant to state law, based on the outcome of the state's popular vote, were those pledged to support Biden, and these electors dutifully cast their ballots for Biden and properly proceeded to send their votes to Congress to be counted on January 6, 2021, as required by the Constitution's Twelfth Amendment. In contrast, the supposed electoral votes cast for Trump had no official status in any of the states because no institution of state government recognized Trump rather than Biden as having won the popular vote in that state. Mike Pence, as Senate President, would not even let these pro-Trump submissions be

---

240 Ibid.

241 United States of America v. Donald J. Trump, Indictment No. 23 CR 257, United States District Court, District of Columbia, August 1, 2023

opened in the joint session of Congress because, without any claim of any backing from any part of their state's government, they could not be acknowledged as even asserting to be official electoral votes entitled to be considered by Congress."[242]

Foley continues; "Since then, the question has arisen whether anyone should be criminally prosecuted in connection with these submissions of groundless pro-Trump electoral votes... there are reasons to be wary of prosecuting any claimed electoral votes sent to Congress... the better course seemingly would be to reject frivolous claims as unworthy of serious consideration...rather than by endeavoring to imprison these frivolous claimants for asserting their preposterous arguments."[243]

Foley notes that there have been other instances of alternate Elector votes being submitted to Congress. "In 1876, South Carolina was one of three southern states that quickly became disputed after the popular vote had been cast in November. Florida and Louisiana were the other two. The Republican candidate, Rutherford Hayes, needed all three of these states for an Electoral College victory, whereas Samuel Tilden needed just one...In South Carolina...there was no one with any colorable claim of official authority in a position to certify Tilden the winner. Still, Democrats there were claiming that he had won...Tilden's electors met and voted for him on the congressional designated day for Electoral College balloting. They submitted their spurious electoral votes to the Senate President pursuant to the Twelfth Amendment as though they rather than the Hayes electors were entitled to cast the state's official Electoral College votes...

"Whatever else was contested during the entire Hayes-Tilden dispute, there was no doubt that the South Carolina electoral votes cast for Tilden were not valid because the individuals who cast them clearly had not been, despite any claims to the contrary, appointed as the state's electors. The Electoral Commission that Congress created to settle the Hayes-Tilden dispute...agreed unanimously...that the individuals in South Carolina who purported to cast electoral votes for Tilden 'were not the lawful electors for the State of South Carolina, and that their votes are not the votes provided for by the

---

[242] Edward B. Foley, Just Security, "A Historical Perspective on Alternate Electors: Lessons from Hayes-Tiden", July 7, 2022

[243] Ibid.

Constitution of the United States and should not be counted.'"[244]

Most important to our current analysis, "[d]espite this unanimity, reflecting the patent invalidity of [the alternate South Carolina electors'] claim to be the state's 'duly and legally appointed' electors, none of these South Carolina individuals...were criminally investigated or prosecuted for making this assertion." In fact, "a couple of years later, during a congressional investigation, evidence emerged that top participants in the Tilden campaign, including Tilden's own nephew, had engaged in an effort to bribe local election officials in the disputed Southern states, including South Carolina, to alter the election returns. But even this apparent criminality did not result in prosecutions and convictions of the perpetrators, but instead caused Tilden's political disgrace, preventing him from returning as the Democratic party's presidential nominee in 1880 as had been his plan immediately after Hayes was inaugurated."[245]

Then, there is this more recent example; "In 2016, Hillary Clinton won the popular vote by 2.9 million votes, but lost the Electoral College to Donald Trump. Prior to the Electoral College vote, which Trump was expected to win 306-232, some progressive Democrats proposed getting Republican electors to switch their votes to Clinton or another Republican on the grounds Trump was unfit for office. The effort ultimately failed, as expected, with Trump winning 304-227 after five Clinton electors and two Trump electors switched votes and took on the mantle of 'faithless electors' - electors who cast a vote for someone other than their party's nominee. The effort cost Clinton more electoral votes than it did Trump."[246]

Under the procedures enacted by the states, for the most part, these Electors were duty-bound to cast their vote for the candidate they were nominated to elect. Yet, contrary to the law, "progressive Democrats" made an effort, in some cases successfully, to convince those Electors to violate the law and their oaths. Were any of these "progressive Democrats" prosecuted for using "unlawful means of discounting legitimate votes and subverting the election results?"

Of course not. Most federal prosecutors have better things to do than become involved in a political process and prosecute "invalid

---

244 Ibid.

245 Ibid.

246 Joseph A. Gambardello, FactCheck.org, "Post Misleadingly Equates 2016 Democratic Effort to Trump's 2020 'Alternate Electors'", June 29, 2022

electors" whose votes have been rejected by Congress, or those who encouraged the submission of those alternate votes.

Thus, if it's not necessarily illegal to submit alternate elector votes, were the means Trump used to gather these alternate Electors "fraudulent?" According to Smith's "January 6" Indictment, "[s]ome fraudulent electors were tricked into participating based on the understanding that their votes would be used only if the Defendant succeeded in outcome-determinative lawsuits within their state, which the Defendant never did." In particular, Smith cites to Arizona, where Trump "falsely asserted...that a substantial number of non-citizens, non-residents, and dead people had voted fraudulently in Arizona." Based on this belief, the former President "asked the Arizona House Speaker to call the legislature into session to hold a hearing based on their claims of election fraud. The Arizona House Speaker refused."[247]

According to Smith's Indictment, "[o]n the morning of January 4, 2021, [one of Trump's attorneys] called the Arizona House Speaker to urge him to use a majority of the legislature to decertify the state's legitimate electors. Arizona's validly ascertained electors had voted three weeks earlier and sent their votes to Congress, which was scheduled to count those votes in Biden's favor in just two days' time at the January 6 certification proceeding...the Arizona House Speaker explained that state investigations had uncovered no evidence of substantial fraud in the state..[t]he Arizona House Speaker refused [decertification], stating that he would not 'play with the oath' he had taken to uphold the United States Constitution and Arizona law."[248]

Yet, where exactly is the "fraudulent" activity on the part of Trump here?

It is true that the Arizona Attorney General conducted an audit of mail-in ballots and determined that a "hand recount of ballots showed Joe Biden won the election in Maricopa County, cementing his win in Arizona." However, that audit also showed "issues with duplicate ballots and chain of custody identified by Senate liaison and former Arizona Secretary of State Ken Bennett as matters the AG should take up." These included problems "found with Maricopa County's voter rolls, such as 5,047 voters who may have cast ballots

---

[247] United States of America v. Donald J. Trump, Indictment No. 23 CR 257, United States District Court, District of Columbia, August 1, 2023

[248] Ibid.

in more than one county; voters with incomplete names, and 198 people who registered to vote after the Oct. 15 cutoff date but nonetheless cast a ballot."[249]

In fact, in September of this year, Arizona Superior Court Judge John Napper ruled that "state law requires county recorders to match mail-ballot signatures with signatures in the voter's 'registration record,' the Secretary instructed them to use a broader and less reliable universe of comparison signatures. That means the Secretary was requiring ballots to be counted despite using a signature that did not match anything in the voter's registration record. This was a clear violation of state law."[250]

In other words, Arizona "is conducting signature matching in an unlawful manner," which would tend to support former President Trump's assertion that" a substantial number of non-citizens, non-residents, and dead people had voted fraudulently in Arizona."

Is the fact that Arizona was using an illegal method of verifying the signatures on mail-in votes conclusive proof of election fraud at a substantial enough level to have altered the results of the 2020 Presidential election? Not in and of itself. But would such evidence provide some basis for a reasonable belief that a further investigation is necessary, and that the certification of the election results by Arizona was premature?

Of course, it would. But despite this evidence, Jack Smith asserts that Trump's actions were "fraudulent" and intended to "subvert" the results of the 2020 Presidential election.

Let us give the last word on this issue to Hugh Hewitt, writing in *The Washington Post*; "Smith might have a much harder time proving his case than he and Trump's many and most vociferous detractors realize... When the 'beyond a reasonable doubt' standard is applied, I don't see a conviction on any of the charges Smith leveled."[251]

---

[249] Mary Jo Pitzl, and Jen Fifield, USA Today, "Arizona Senate leaders confirm Biden win but call for further review of election procedures", September 24, 2021
[250] Pamela Geller, Geller Report, "Arizona Judge Rules CURRENT Mail-In Ballot Process Unlawful, Violated the Law In Both 2020 & 2022 Elections, Half A Million Ballots Fraudulent", September 7, 2023
[251] Hugh Hewitt, The Washington Post, "Opinion: Why the Trump Jan. 6 indictment will fail", August 8, 2023

16 DONALD TRUMP CANNOT GET A FAIR TRIAL FROM JUDGE TANYA CHUTKAN

"At its core, the invocation of 'judicial impartiality' in political discourse speaks to an ideal of fairness: an impartial judge is a person who acts in a fair manner toward all parties in a case appearing before them." Stuart Chinn, University of Oregon School of Law[252]

One of the basic requirements in our system of justice is the necessity for an impartial judge. In fact, "Canon 3E/Rule 2.11[a] of the model code of judicial conduct creates a general requirement for disqualification whenever a judge's 'impartiality might reasonably be questioned.'" The model code of judicial conduct even lists "specific examples of circumstances in which a judge's impartiality might reasonably be questioned." These include a requirement for disqualification "if the judge has...a personal bias or prejudice concerning a party or a party's lawyer."[253]

It would seem that this rule of professional conduct now includes this proviso; "unless the party to be tried is Donald J. Trump."

In chapter 3, we discussed Federal Magistrate Judge Bruce Reinhart, who signed the search warrant for the FBI allowing the raid on Mar A Lago, despite having recused himself from hearing a civil case brought by the former President just months earlier. We noted there that "[t]he statute...the magistrate cited for his recusal states in

---

[252] Stuart Chinn, (2020) "The Meaning of Judicial Impartiality: An Examination of Supreme Court Confirmation Debates and Supreme Court Rulings on Racial Equality," Utah Law Review: Vol. 2019: No. 5, Article 1

[253] Ibid.

part that a judge 'shall disqualify himself in any proceeding in which his impartiality might reasonably be questioned' and then describes the various circumstances that could trigger such concerns. They include 'a personal bias or prejudice concerning a party, or personal knowledge of disputed evidentiary facts or prior work as a lawyer for a party involved in the case. Reinhart's order did not specify the conflict or source of his concern for recusal."

Apparently, Magistrate Reinhart felt he could not be fair in listening to a case brought by former President Trump, but he had no problem with allowing federal agents to search the former First Ladies' underwear draw, as well as the rest of the Trump's Florida residence.

Reinhart is not the only clearly biased judge who has been called upon to decide the fate of Donald Trump. In this Chapter we consider the judge appointed to hear Special Counsel Jack Smith's Second Federal Indictment of the former President - Washington DC District Court Judge Tanya Chutkan.

According to the DC District Court's webpage, "Chutkan was appointed to the United States District Court for the District of Columbia in June 2014. Born in Kingston, Jamaica, she received her B.A. in Economics from George Washington University and her J.D. from the University of Pennsylvania Law School."[254] A former Public Defender, Judge Chutkan specialized in white collar crime and antitrust litigation after she left the Public Defender's Office.

Coincidentally, she just happens to be the judge who has handled the majority of defendants arrested and prosecuted as a result of the Capitol Riot on January 6, 2021. As reported by *NBC News*, "Chutkan, an Obama appointee who has served on the bench for nearly a decade, quickly established a reputation for imposing some of the toughest penalties on rioters who participated in the 2021 attack on the Capitol. In December 2021, Chutkan gave what was then the longest sentence — just over five years — to a Florida man who had been charged with dispensing a fire extinguisher and throwing it at police during the attack. 'It has to be made clear that trying to violently overthrow the government, trying to stop the peaceful transition of power, and assaulting law enforcement officers in that effort is going to be met with absolutely certain punishment,'

---

[254] Website, United States District Court, District of Columbia, District Judge Tanya S. Chutkan

Chutkan said at the time."[255]

There is no question that someone who throws a fire extinguisher at police officers deserves a jail sentence. But notice the language used by Judge Chutkan; she clearly indicates her belief that the Capitol Riot was a violent attempt to overthrow the government, not a demonstration that got out of hand.

However, "[a]ccording to an analysis from NPR's investigative team, as of July 2023, Chutkan had given prison sentences to all of the 38 Jan. 6 defendants to come before her, even though prosecutors had only recommended 34 of them for prison. That stands in contrast to the other judges in Jan. 6 cases who have tended to be more lenient at sentencing."[256]

If Chutkan thinks the January 6 riot was an attempt to overthrow the government of the United States, who does she believe is responsible for that day's events?

According to the *Longville News Journal*, "[a] review of thousands of pages of hearing transcripts reveal that Chutkan has repeatedly expressed strong and settled opinions about the issues at the heart of *United States v. Donald Trump* – the criminal case she is now presiding over. These include her public assertions...that the Jan. 6 protests were orchestrated by Trump, and that the former president is guilty of crimes. She has described Jan. 6 as a 'mob attack' on 'the very foundation of our democracy' and branded the issue at the heart of the case she is hearing – Trump's claim that the 2020 election was stolen – a conspiracy theory."[257]

Further, "[b]efore sentencing Christine Priola, a Trump supporter from Ohio who pleaded guilty to obstruction of an official proceeding, to 15 months in jail, Chutkan appeared to lament the fact Trump was not yet in prison. '[The] people who mobbed that Capitol were there in fealty, in loyalty, to one man – not to the Constitution, of which most of the people who come before me seem woefully ignorant, not to the ideals of this country, and not to the principles of

---

[255] Zoe Richards, NBC News, "Who is Tanya Chutkan, the judge assigned to Trump's election case?", August 2, 2023

[256] Carrie Johnson, NPR, "Judge in Trump trial has a tough sentencing record in Jan. 6 cases", August 25, 2023

[257] Julie Kelly, Longville News Journal, "In Her Jan. 6 Courtroom, Judge Who Will Hear Trump's Case Is the Pot Calling the Defendant Incendiary", October 26, 2023

democracy,' Chutkan said on Oct. 28, 2022. 'It's a blind loyalty to one person who, by the way, *remains free to this day.'* (Emphasis added.)"[258]

In the case of Matthew Mazzocco, "another Jan. 6 defendant, [Chutkan rejected] Mazzocco's argument that he traveled from Texas to Washington to engage in a legal political demonstration [and] declared at his October 2021 sentencing hearing: 'He went there to support one man who he viewed had the election taken from him. In total disregard of a lawfully conducted election, he went to the Capitol in support of one man, not in support of our country or in support of democracy.' Although Mazzocco only spent 12 minutes inside the Capitol and committed no violence, Chutkan rejected the government's recommendation of three months home confinement for pleading guilty to "parading" in the Capitol, a Class B misdemeanor, and instead sentenced Mazzocco to 45 days in jail."[259]

In other words, the Judge who has publicly stated that "one man" disregarded "a lawfully conducted election" and that this "one man" is responsible for "an attack on the very foundation of our democracy," who also calls the January 6 riot "an attempt to overthrow the government" is now the Judge assigned to hear charges brought against that one man, arising out of the events of January 6 - Donald J. Trump.

Obviously, the former President's lawyers also know that a judge "who's impartiality might reasonably be questioned," should recuse themselves from hearing that case. In that regard, a motion was made before Judge Chutkan, asking that these charges be heard by another judge. Her response?

"U.S. District Judge Tanya Chutkan said...she won't recuse herself from Donald Trump's 2020 election interference case in Washington, rejecting the former president's claims that her past comments raise doubts about whether she can be fair... In seeking Chutkan's recusal, defense lawyers cited statements she had made in two sentencing hearings of participants in the Jan. 6, 2021 riot at the U.S. Capitol in which they said she had appeared to suggest that Trump deserved to be prosecuted and held accountable. They said the comments suggested a bias against him that could taint the proceedings. But Chutkan vigorously objected to those characterizations of her comments. 'It bears noting that the court has never taken the

---

258 Ibid.

259 Ibid.

position the defense ascribes to it: that former "President Trump should be prosecuted and imprisoned," Chutkan wrote. 'And the defense does not cite any instance of the court ever uttering those words or anything similar.'"[260]

Yes, you read that right. In the past, Judge Chutkan has stated that one man, who remains free, is responsible for the January 6th "attempt to overthrow the government," based on that one man's refusal to accept the results of a "lawfully conducted" election. But because she never actually identified that one man by name, she believes she can be fair.

Even while she has imposed harsher sentences than most of her judicial brethren on the people she believes followed that one man.

Maybe Judge Chutkan believes this nonsense. Maybe she can compartmentalize her views from the evidence she hears, and maybe she can give Donald Trump a fair trial.

Maybe.

But what this judge has forgotten, is that the obligation to be fair and impartial is only part of a Court's obligation. A judge is also required to avoid the appearance of partiality. According to Cannon 2 of the Code of Conduct for United States Judges, "[a] Judge Should Avoid Impropriety and the Appearance of Impropriety in all Activities...[a]n appearance of impropriety occurs when reasonable minds, with knowledge of all the relevant circumstances disclosed by a reasonable inquiry, would conclude that the judge's honesty, integrity, impartiality, temperament, or fitness to serve as a judge is impaired."[261]

In practice, the requirement to avoid the appearance of unfairness and bias is stronger than the necessity to avoid actual partiality and prejudice. "A federal district judge who spoke to a newspaper to clarify procedural matters should have recused herself from the case because her comments could have been interpreted to indicate that she was biased, even though the judge in no way abdicated her ethical responsibilities by speaking, the U.S. Court of Appeals in Boston (1st Cir.) ruled on February. 5, [2001]...the court found that [the judge]

---

[260] Alanna Durkin Richer, and Eric Tucker, AP News, "Judge Chutkan denies Trump's request to recuse herself in federal election subversion case", September 27, 2023

[261] Code of Conduct for United States Judges, Canon 2, Commentary, Canon 2A, effective March 12, 2019

should have recused herself because a reader might interpret her comments as evidence of bias. Even though she did not violate judicial ethics, the court said just a perception of bias was sufficient for recusal."[262]

Judge Chutkan has made a series of statements in a number of cases where she has handed out tough sentences to January 6th defendants, laying the blame for their conduct on the one man who now stands before her seeking a fair and impartial hearing. Even if she can separate her personal animosity from her obligation to hear the case with an unbiased ear, who truly believes she will actually give Donald Trump a fair trial?

---

[262] Anonymous, Reporters Committee For Freedom of the Press, "Judge's public comments warrant recusal", February 21, 2001

17 "TRUMP'S BIGGEST LEGAL CHALLENGE YET"

In Chapters 5 through 7, we discussed Manhattan District Attorney Alvin Bragg's indictment of Donald Trump. Then, in Chapters 8 through 10 we dissected Special Counsel Jack Smith's first federal indictment of the former President. In Chapter 11, we also reviewed the facts and charges Smith added to this first federal indictment. Next, in Chapters 13 through 15, we analyzed Smith's second federal indictment of the 45th President.

Two federal indictments, one in Florida and another in Washington DC, as well as a New York City indictment would all be a heavy burden for any defendant, especially one who is running for President of the United States.

But wait - there's more.

On August 14, 2023, "[f]ormer President Donald Trump was indicted...on racketeering, conspiracy and other charges by a grand jury in Fulton County, Georgia, the result of a more than two-year investigation...into potential 2020 election interference in that state. Eighteen other people, including Trump's former lawyer Rudy Giuliani and former White House chief of staff Mark Meadows, were also indicted, accused of joining Trump in efforts to unlawfully change the outcome of the election."[263]

Specifically, Trump and his co-defendants are alleged to have "unlawfully conspired and endeavored to conduct and participate in...a pattern of racketeering activity" while "associated with an enterprise" that allegedly violated Georgia law...Trump and the other

[263] Hannah Grabenstein, PBS, "Read the full Georgia indictment against Trump and 18 allies", August 15, 2023

defendants charged in this Indictment refused to accept that Trump had lost [the 2020 Presidential election], and they knowingly and willfully joined a conspiracy to unlawfully change the outcome of the election in favor of Trump."[264]

As described by *PBS*, "[t]he nearly 100-page indictment details dozens of acts by Trump or his allies to undo his defeat, including beseeching Georgia's Republican secretary of state to find enough votes for him to win the battleground state; harassing an election worker who faced false claims of fraud; and attempting to persuade Georgia lawmakers to ignore the will of voters and appoint a new slate of electoral college electors favorable to Trump."[265]

"The yearslong probe of former President Donald Trump and his allies by Fulton County, Georgia, District Attorney Fani Willis may prove to be Trump's toughest legal challenge yet," *ABC News* breathlessly reports. Yet, despite their obvious glee at yet another Trump indictment, the mainstream media seems to recognize that the shine is off the apple here. "What was once unprecedented -- a former president facing criminal charges -- has fallen into a familiar cadence...Trump and his campaign will decry the charges. His campaign will likely fundraise off of these charges. Trump and his campaign continue to conflate his personal legal problems with the cause of his political movement, using the charges as a tool to gin up his base. It has been working. Numerous charges haven't slowed his campaign yet."[266]

You can hear the disappointment loud and clear - "Darn it! Won't anything stop this man?"

Donald Trump is a human being, not a relentless Juggernaut. Certainly, something, or some event (such as several losses in upcoming primaries) could potentially "stop him." But this indictment by another local prosecutor, this time in Fulton County, Georgia, isn't likely to cause the derailment of the runaway Trump train.

Who has brought this latest Indictment against the former

---

[264] State of Georgia v. Donald J. Trump, et al., Indictment filed August 14, 2023, Fulton County Superior Court, Georgia

[265] Kate Brumback and Eric Tucker, PBS, "Trump and 18 allies indicted in Georgia 2020 election case", August 15, 2023

[266] Averi Harper, ABC News, "Sweeping indictment could be Trump's biggest legal challenge yet: ANALYSIS", August 15, 2023

President? According to the *BBC*, Fulton County, Georgia District Attorney Fani Willis was born "in Inglewood, California in 1971 [and] was raised primarily by her father, a criminal defense lawyer and member of the Black Panthers, the radical political party which championed black rights...[s]he graduated from the historically black college Howard University in 1993, before receiving a law degree from Emory University in Georgia in 1996...Ms Willis joined the Fulton County District Attorney's office, where she served in several different divisions until 2018..[a]fter her time in the office ended, Ms Willis spent several years in private practice. Then, in 2020, she decided to go head-to-head with her former boss, six-term Fulton County District Attorney Paul Howard. She won in a runoff election with 73% of the votes, becoming the first black woman to serve as Fulton County's top prosecutor."[267]

Unlike the Manhattan DA, Alvin Bragg, who "received more than $1 million in support from the Color Of Change PAC, a racial justice group which receives funding from [George] Soros" during his campaign,[268] there isn't any clear evidence that Willis is yet another "progressive DA". Her office's website includes a pledge to "provide an environment of mutual respect, regardless of race, color, religion, sex, national origin, sexual orientation, age, disability or gender identity," however, there is also a statement of integrity, which reads "this office will now show a consistent and uncompromising adherence to strong moral and ethical principles and values."[269]

Further, unlike Bragg, who specifically campaigned on his plan "to personally focus on the high-profile probe into former President Donald Trump's business practices,"[270] there is scant evidence that Willis made similar overt promises during her race.[271]

What Willis does bring to this prosecution is a willingness to use racketeering charges indiscriminately against any and all defendants.

---

[267] Madeline Halpert, BBC, "Who is Fani Willis, the prosecutor taking on Donald Trump in Georgia?", August 15, 2023

[268] Alex Oliveira, Daily Mail, "George Soros' man in the Manhattan DA's office: Billionaire Dem donor funded Alvin Bragg's campaign to the tune of $1million while he promised to put Trump behind bars", March 20, 2023

[269] Website, Fulton County Georgia, District Attorney, Core Values

[270] Kara Scannell, CNN, "New Manhattan DA Alvin Bragg pledges to focus on Trump investigations", December 20, 2021

[271] Amy Sherman, Politifact, "Did Fulton County DA Fani Willis campaign to 'get Trump'? No, she didn't say that", August 18, 2023/

In fact, it would seem that Willis only carries one hammer, which makes every criminal case look like a nail to her.

Similar to the federal RICO (Racketeer Influenced and Corrupt Organizations) law, under Georgia Code Section 16-14-4, "[a] It shall be unlawful for any person, through a pattern of racketeering activity or proceeds derived therefrom, to acquire or maintain, directly or indirectly, any interest in or control of any enterprise, real property, or personal property of any nature, including money. (b) It shall be unlawful for any person employed by or associated with any enterprise to conduct or participate in, directly or indirectly, such enterprise through a pattern of racketeering activity. (c) It shall be unlawful for any person to conspire or endeavor to violate any of the provisions of subsection (a) or (b) of this Code section."

What is "racketeering activity" under Georgia law? "Racketeering is defined as, the illegal use of force, violence, or economic or political power to control or extort an enterprise. In the context of Georgia law, it is illegal to engage in a pattern of activity that includes at least two acts of racketeering activity within a 10 year period. The activities may include bribery, extortion, fraud, obstructing justice, counterfeiting, and trafficking in stolen property, among others." Further, "[i]n Georgia, racketeering is a felony charge, and is punishable by significant fines and up to ten years in prison."[272]

The Georgia RICO statute has been a formidable weapon in Fani Willis' arsenal. "[i]n 2013, Willis turned heads in one of her first big cases: She helped convene a grand jury that indicted decorated [Atlanta Schools] Superintendent Beverly Hall and nearly three dozen other educators for cheating on state standardized tests...Hall, the Atlanta superintendent, arrived in the district in 1999, eventually leading what she would call a data-driven turnaround...[b]y 2009...the Journal-Constitution published the first of several stories analyzing Atlanta's results on the Georgia Criterion-Referenced Competency Test. The analysis found that scores had risen at rates that were statistically 'all but impossible.' It also found that district officials disregarded internal irregularities and retaliated against whistleblowers."[273]

---

[272] Scott Hamlin, legalopedia, "Racketeering / RICO in Georgia: Legal Definition, Things to Know", undated

[273] Greg Toppo, Yahoo News, "Before Trump, D.A. Fani Willis Targeted Teachers in Atlanta Cheating Scandal", August 18, 2023

As described by *Yahoo News*, "[c]ritics would soon compare Hall to 'a Mafia boss who demanded fealty from subordinates while perpetrating a massive, self-serving fraud,' the city newspaper reported at the time. Willis pursued Hall using the same tools many prosecutors employ against Mafia bosses and drug kingpins. In bringing charges under the state's RICO Act, Willis alleged that Hall and her colleagues used the 'legitimate enterprise' of the school system to carry out an illegitimate act: cheating."[274]

Was this use of the RICO statute effective? Public opinion on the case was sharply divided, with many Black commentators accusing Willis of overreach. But eventually, 34 of Hall's subordinates faced criminal charges...[w]hile most of the Atlanta educators eventually pleaded guilty to avoid jail time, 12 went to trial in 2014...[t]he jury convicted 11 of the 12 of racketeering and other charges."[275]

What of the "Atlanta Schools kingpin", Superintendent Beverly Hall? "Hall retired in 2011 [and] died of breast cancer in 2015, at age 68."[276]

More recently, "[i]n the spring of 2022, (Young Thug) the rapper - full name Jeffrey Lamar Williams - was charged alongside 27 of his alleged affiliates with 56 violations of Georgia's (RICO) Act. He's been cast by prosecutors as the criminal mastermind of Young Slime Life, a gang prosecutors claim was active from 2012. It was a shocking development for fans of Thug, a hugely popular artist and one of the most influential rappers of his generation. He faces up to 40 years in prison."[277]

One of the more unique features of Willis' prosecution of Young Thug and his co-defendants is her use of "the Thugger lyrics, 'I'm prepared to take them down' and 'I never killed anybody but I got something to do with that body'...Willis...said she would [also] be leaning on lyrics in another RICO case prosecuting 26 alleged members of the Drug Rich Gang, who are charged with kidnappings, armed robberies, shootings and high-profile home invasions. Among the targeted were singer Mariah Carey, Atlanta Falcons wide receiver Calvin Ridley and Atlanta United goalkeeper Brad Guzan, according

[274] Ibid.

[275] Ibid.

[276] Ibid.

[277] Walden Green and Raphael Helfand, The Fader, "Young Thug and the YSL RICO trial, explained", September 12, 2023

to a 220-count indictment. 'I think if you decide to admit your crimes over a beat, I'm going to use it,' she said, deflecting criticism. 'I'm not targeting anyone, but however, you do not get to commit crimes in my county and then decide to brag on it.'"[278]

These indictments have also received their fair share of criticism. "RICO is most commonly used as a tactic to sweep up entire street gangs," according to Sidney Madden, the co-host of a podcast for *NPR* entitled *Louder than a Riot.* [t]he definition of a street gang gets real spongy when you look at it in Black communities. When prosecutors apply RICO to rap, it's not just the rappers getting caught up in the system, but it's their whole crew and their whole entourage. Everyone is being roped in and classified as a gang member. Basically, it allows prosecutors to hold anyone and everyone in an entire group responsible for the worst things someone in their circle has done. So if you're a rapper and you associate with people engaging in criminal activity — maybe y'all grew up on the same block, maybe you used to run the same streets before you switched into entertainment, maybe you brought them with you out of the streets into entertainment — prosecutors can use all that and use RICO laws to brand y'all as an organized crime syndicate."[279]

Substitute the word "rapper" for "Trump campaign worker" or "Trump attorney," and the basis for DA Willis' RICO charges against Trump and his "entourage" become clear - "everyone is being roped in and classified as a gang member."

According to Joe Lancaster, writing for *Reason*, "Willis is unapologetic about her use of the statute, saying in August 2022, 'I'm a fan of RICO'...[she noted that] her office has pursued 11 RICO cases since she became D.A. in January 2021. She has primarily used it against gangs, bringing RICO charges in 2022 and 2023 over a series of Atlanta shootings and home invasions."[280]

But is this necessarily a good thing? "RICO statutes allow prosecutors to bring charges using guilt by association. Kerry Martin

---

[278] Eliott C. McLaughlin, CNN, "Atlanta-area prosecutor cites rap lyrics as evidence, which hip-hop has long decried as a double standard", August 31, 2022

[279] Sidney Madden et al., NPR, "The charges against Young Thug build on a growing trend of criminalizing rap crews", May 15, 2022

[280] Lancaster, Joe, Reason, "Fani Willis Is Abusing Georgia's Terrible RICO Law", August 16, 2023

wrote in the *Michigan Journal of Race & Law* that RICO 'is not supposed to criminalize mere membership in a gang, but it comes dangerously close to doing so.'"[281]

Lancaster continues: "The original federal RICO law was drafted for use against the mafia, allowing prosecutors to bring conspiracy charges based on certain predicate acts. It quickly expanded to include all manner of activity that was already illegal but could now be charged more aggressively. As *Reason* noted all the way back in 1990, 'Ambitious federal prosecutors have now discovered RICO's many uses, and this poses a great danger to civil liberty and free enterprise.' Georgia's RICO law is even more expansive than its federal counterpart - for example, it does not require multiple defendants or an extended timeline to establish a conspiracy. Former prosecutor Chris Timmons told *ABC News*, 'Somebody could go to JC Penney, shoplift a pair of socks, walk next door to Sears and shoplift a second pair of socks, and they can be charged with RICO.'"[282]

In other words, Willis routinely takes advantage of a very broad statute to bring conspiracy charges against large groups, and spends years wearing down those accused of being members of those groups, just as she did with the Atlanta school system, and is currently doing with Young Thug and his associates. "Thug has been in Cobb County Jail since May of [2022]. He spent his first eight months there awaiting the proposed January 9 start date of his court proceedings and has remained there for the past eight while Fulton County Superior Court Judge Ural Glanville continues to conduct extensive juror search that's set to make the YSL trial the longest in Georgia history."[283]

With the next Presidential election scheduled to be held in less than a year, can there be any doubt that the Fulton County DA wishes to keep Donald Trump and his campaign "organization" tied up in complex litigation for the foreseeable future?

---

281 Ibid.
282 Ibid.
283 Walden Green and Raphael Helfand, The Fader, "Young Thug and the YSL RICO trial, explained", September 12, 2023

18 DEJA VU ALL OVER AGAIN

The late Hall of Fame catcher for the New York Yankees, Yogi Berra, was famous for his "unique and witty observations" such as "nobody goes there anymore. It's too crowded," and "when you come to a fork in the road, take it."[284] He also claimed, "I didn't really say everything I said," however, there is one phrase Yogi coined that applies to the Indictment filed by Fulton County, Georgia District Attorney Fani Willis against former President Donald Trump; "It's deja vu all over again."

In Chapter 13, we discussed the similarity between the second impeachment of the 45th President and the charges brought by Special Counsel Jack Smith in his second federal indictment of Donald Trump.[285] A review of the indictment brought by Willis shows a strong identity between many of the "criminal" acts alleged by Smith, and those cited by Willis.[286]

Unfortunately for former President Trump, it is perfectly legal for a state prosecutor to bring charges under state law for the same or similar conduct that is the subject of a federal prosecution, or *vice versa.* As stated by University of Georgia law professor John Meixner, a former assistant U.S. attorney, "the federal and state are...separate sovereigns where each can do what they choose."[287]

---

[284] Yogi Berra Museum & Learning Center, "Yogi-isms", undated

[285] United States of America v. Donald J. Trump, Indictment No. 23 CR 257, United States District Court, District of Columbia, August 1, 2023

[286] State of Georgia v. Donald J. Trump, et al., Indictment filed August 14, 2023, Fulton County Superior Court, Georgia

[287] Peter Grier, Patrik Jonsson, and Henry Gass, Christian Science Monitor, "At

Granted, there are also significant differences between the Georgia Indictment and Smith's federal charges. While Smith charges Trump, and Trump alone, with several counts of Conspiracy, Willis' takes the extra step of using Georgia's Racketeer Influenced and Corrupt Organizations Act (RICO) to prosecute Trump and 18 "co-conspirators." Smith notes there are "unindicted co-conspirators," but he does not name or charge them in his indictment.

As was noted in the last Chapter, under Georgia Code Section 16-14-4, "[a] It shall be unlawful for any person, through a pattern of racketeering activity or proceeds derived therefrom, to acquire or maintain, directly or indirectly, any interest in or control of any enterprise, real property, or personal property of any nature, including money. (b) It shall be unlawful for any person employed by or associated with any enterprise to conduct or participate in, directly or indirectly, such enterprise through a pattern of racketeering activity. (c) It shall be unlawful for any person to conspire or endeavor to violate any of the provisions of subsection (a) or (b) of this Code section."

We also noted that under Georgia law, "Racketeering is defined as the illegal use of force, violence, or economic or political power to control or extort an enterprise. In the context of Georgia law, it is illegal to engage in a pattern of activity that includes at least two acts of racketeering activity within a 10 year period. The activities may include bribery, extortion, fraud, obstructing justice, counterfeiting, and trafficking in stolen property, among others."[288]

There are 41 counts alleged in the Georgia indictment, 13 of which specifically name the former President. These include the violation of the Georgia RICO statute, "Solicitation of Violation of Oath by Public Official," "Conspiracy to Commit Impersonating a Public Official," "Conspiracy to Commit Forgery," "Conspiracy to Commit False Statements and Writings," "Filing False Documents," and making "False Statements and Writings." Trump is alleged to have "unlawfully conspired and endeavored to conduct and participate in, directly and indirectly, [an] enterprise through [a] pattern of racketeering activity."[289]

---

heart of Jan. 6 case: Trump's state of mind", August 2, 2023

[288] Scott Hamlin, legalopedia, "Racketeering / RICO in Georgia: Legal Definition, Things to Know", undated

In defining the "racketeering enterprise," the Fulton County DA alleges that "[t]he enterprise constituted an ongoing organization whose members and associates functioned as [a] continuing unit for [the] common purpose of achieving the objectives of the enterprise. The enterprise operated in Fulton County, Georgia, elsewhere in the State of Georgia, in other states, including, but not limited to, Arizona, Michigan, Nevada, New Mexico, Pennsylvania, and Wisconsin, and in the District of Columbia. The enterprise operated for [a] period of time sufficient to permit its members and associates to pursue its objectives."[290]

This explanation sounds very much like the description for a perfectly legal organization - Donald Trump's 2020 re-election committee - with a perfectly legal goal - the re-election of the President.

This is one of the issues that brings the most criticism to the overbroad Georgia RICO statute - ANY organization could fit the bill of a "racketeering enterprise." But under the statute, it is the actions of the members of the enterprise that make it a criminal organization, not its structure alone.

What acts committed by Donald Trump are alleged to have been done in furtherance of the conspiracy?

First and foremost is Trump's claim that he won the 2020 Presidential election. Allegedly, he made this claim knowing that he had not won. "On or about the 4th day of November 2020," the Georgia Indictment reads, "DONALD JOHN TRUMP made [a] nationally televised speech falsely declaring victory in the 2020 presidential election." How do the prosecutors know this statement to have been false? "Approximately four days earlier, on or about October 31, 2020, DONALD JOHN TRUMP discussed [a] draft speech with unindicted coconspirator Individual l, whose identity is known to the Grand Jury, that falsely declared victory and falsely claimed voter fraud. The speech was an overt act in furtherance of the conspiracy."[291]

In other words, it is alleged that Trump gave his speech on November 4, *knowing* that his claims of victory were false. Yet, there

---

[289] State of Georgia v. Donald J. Trump, et al., Indictment filed August 14, 2023, Fulton County Superior Court, Georgia

[290] Ibid.

[291] Ibid.

is no proof offered for this assertion. The reference to the "unindicted co-conspirator" is either a "red herring" or a misstatement - just because Trump discussed his proposed election night speech with someone days before he gave it doesn't mean Trump was going to falsely claim he won. It could just as easily mean that the former President anticipated victory.

What exactly did Trump say that night? "It's...clear that we have won Georgia. We're up by 2.5% or 117,000 votes with only 7% left. They're never going to catch us. They can't catch us...We also, if you look and you see Arizona, we have a lot of life in that. And somebody declared that it was a victory for… And maybe it will be. I mean, that's possible...certainly there were a lot of votes out there that we could get because we're now just coming into what they call Trump territory. I don't know what you call it. But these were friendly Trump voters. And that could be overturned."[292]

Of course, these predictions turned out to be incorrect. But Willis' charges seem more focused on this part of the speech; "[a]ll of a sudden everything just stopped... This is a fraud on the American public. This is an embarrassment to our country. We were getting ready to win this election. Frankly, we did win this election. We did win this election. So, our goal now is to ensure the integrity for the good of this nation. This is a very big moment. This is a major fraud in our nation. We want the law to be used in a proper manner. So we'll be going to the US Supreme Court. We want all voting to stop. We don't want them to find any ballots at four o'clock in the morning and add them to the list. Okay? It's a very sad moment. To me this is a very sad moment and we will win this. And as far as I'm concerned, we already have won it."[293]

Allegations regarding this speech are also made in Smith's second federal indictment; "Despite having lost, the Defendant was determined to remain in power...following election day on November 3, 2020, the Defendant spread lies that there had been outcome-determinative fraud in the election and that he had actually won. These claims were false, and the Defendant knew that they were false."[294]

---

[292] Donald Trump, @rev, "Donald Trump 2020 Election Night Speech Transcript", November 4, 2020

[293] Ibid.

[294] United States of America v. Donald J. Trump, Indictment No. 23 CR 257,

Of course, it is unclear how either prosecutor expects to prove that Donald Trump was not truthful when he made these allegations of fraud. As described by *The Christian Science Monitor*, "Mr. Trump's defense against these...charges will likely rely at least in part on the insistence that he continued to believe these claims, notwithstanding others' objections, and that his actions were thus not corrupt at heart. The outcome of crucial parts of the case could thus depend on a jury's belief about Mr. Trump's state of mind – a difficult judgment when it comes to a man whose career has often involved bombast, stubbornness, and, at the least, a fondness for exaggeration."[295]

Another focus of both indictments is the attempt by the Trump campaign to seek alternate electors for appointment to the Electoral College. According to Smith, the former President and his "co-conspirators organized fraudulent slates of electors in seven targeted states (Arizona, Georgia, Michigan, Nevada, New Mexico, Pennsylvania, and Wisconsin), attempting to mimic the procedures that the legitimate electors were supposed to follow under the Constitution and other federal and state laws. This included causing the fraudulent electors to meet on the day appointed by federal law on which legitimate electors were to gather and cast their votes; cast fraudulent votes for the Defendant; and sign certificates falsely representing that they were legitimate electors."[296]

According to Willis, three members of the Trump "organization and a group of unindicted co-conspirators "committed the felony offense of IMPERSONATING PUBLIC OFFICER...in Fulton County, Georgia, by unlawfully falsely holding themselves out as the duly elected and qualified presidential electors from the State of Georgia, public officers, with intent to mislead the President of the United States Senate...into believing that they actually were such officers by placing in the United States mail to said persons document titled "CERTIFICATE OF THE VOTES OF THE 2020 ELECTORS FROM GEORGIA." This was an act of racketeering activity...and an overt act in furtherance of the conspiracy."[297]

United States District Court, District of Columbia, August 1, 2023

[295] Peter Grier, Patrik Jonsson, and Henry Gass, Christian Science Monitor, "At heart of Jan. 6 case: Trump's state of mind", August 2, 2023

[296] United States of America v. Donald J. Trump, Indictment No. 23 CR 257, United States District Court, District of Columbia, August 1, 2023

[297] State of Georgia v. Donald J. Trump, et al., Indictment filed August 14, 2023,

We have previously discussed the difficulty of criminalizing the political effort to seat alternate electors. In particular we quoted Constitutional Law Professor Ed Foley, who stated that "there are reasons to be wary of prosecuting any claimed electoral votes sent to Congress... the better course seemingly would be to reject frivolous claims as unworthy of serious consideration...rather than by endeavoring to imprison these frivolous claimants for asserting their preposterous arguments."[298]

Then there are the events of January 2, 2021, when Trump famously spoke by telephone with Georgia Secretary of State Brad Raffensperger and "repeatedly asked [him] to 'find' more than 11,000 ballots needed to overcome the gap between Trump and Biden in the state, thereby flipping the state in his favor. 'The people of Georgia are angry, the people in the country are angry. And there's nothing wrong with saying, you know, that you've recalculated,' Trump told Raffensperger before questioning the secretary about a 'rumor' that ballots for him were 'shredded' in Fulton County, which is home to Atlanta, the state's largest city and a major Democratic bastion. 'All I want to do is this,' the president continued. 'I just want to find 11,780 votes, which is one more than we have. Because we won the state.'"[299]

This phone call is charged in the Georgia indictment as Act #112 in furtherance of the "criminal enterprise." Trump is alleged to have engaged in "unlawfully soliciting, requesting, and importuning Georgia Secretary of State Brad Raffensperger, public officer, to engage in conduct constituting the felony offense of Violation of Oath by Public Officer...by unlawfully altering, unlawfully adjusting, and otherwise unlawfully influencing the certified returns for presidential electors for the November 3, 2020, presidential election in Georgia, in willful and intentional violation of the terms of the oath of said person as prescribed by law, with intent that said person engage in said conduct."[300]

This phone call is also described in Smith's indictment as follows:

Fulton County Superior Court, Georgia

298 Edward B. Foley, Just Security, "A Historical Perspective on Alternate Electors: Lessons from Hayes-Tiden", July 7, 2022

299 John Bowden, The Hill, "Trump asked Georgia secretary of state to 'find' 11.7k ballots, recalculate election result", January 3, 2021/

300 State of Georgia v. Donald J. Trump, et al., Indictment filed August 14, 2023, Fulton County Superior Court, Georgia

"[f]our days before Congress's certification proceeding, the Defendant and others called Georgia's Secretary of State. During the call, the Defendant lied to the Georgia Secretary of State to induce him to alter Georgia's popular vote count and call into question the validity of the Biden electors' vote...[t]he Defendant said that he needed to 'find' 11,780 votes, and insinuated that the Georgia Secretary of State and his Counsel could be subject to criminal prosecution if they failed to find election fraud as he demanded."[301]

Yet, there is a more innocent explanation for the January 2 call offered by former federal prosecutor and George Washington University Law Professor Jonathan Turley; "The call Trump participated in was a settlement discussion over election challenges with a variety of lawyers present, not some backroom at the Bada Bing club. The entire stated purpose of the challenges was to count what the Trump campaign alleged were uncounted votes that far surpassed the 11,780 deficit. Trump repeatedly asserted that he won the election and continued to return to the fact that officials only needed to confirm 11,780 of those hundreds of thousands of allegedly uncounted ballots...He was discussing what he viewed as uncounted votes that far exceeded the margin of roughly 12,000 and noting, as part of the request for access to data, that they do not need to find much to overturn the result. In any criminal case, Trump would simply argue that he was restating the point of the pending cases in a settlement negotiation: that the election was not fair and that a review could easily flip the result given the margin."[302]

As to whether or not Trump threatened the Georgia Secretary of State, as Smith asserts, Turley notes that "experts like Anthony Michael Kreis, a professor at the Georgia State University College of Law, declared that Trump's 'only demand is to have votes tossed or invented to fabricate a win' and that 'there's no way to read this other than a blatant attempt to pressure Georgia officials to lie and alter legitimate election results with a wink and a nod to a looming consequence.' But Trump did not actually say that...[any] fraud prosecution would be based on a statement that could be easily defended as part of a settlement discussion without any clear threat

---

[301] United States of America v. Donald J. Trump, Indictment No. 23 CR 257, United States District Court, District of Columbia, August 1, 2023

[302] Jonathan Turley, Fox News, "Jonathan Turley: It's legally absurd to claim Trump committed crime in call with Georgia election officials", January 6, 2021

or benefit discussed...Trump was seeking access to data and his belief that fraudulent, and possible criminal, conduct marred the results. One can reject those claims (as I have) without converting the matter into a faux criminal case."[303]

Turley also reiterates the central issue of both Smith's second federal indictment, and Willis' charges; "A prosecutor would have to show that Trump clearly knew his theories were bogus and that he did not believe there were sufficient ballots to reach that number."[304]

In general, then, much of Trump's defense will be the same in both of these cases. Trump will assert that he truly believed he won the election, and that he believed there to be widespread voter fraud in Georgia, and other states, fraud that has continued to be uncovered as time goes on.

There is support for this position. In February of 2021, "Georgia election officials [referred] for possible criminal prosecution a potential voter fraud case involving a group recently linked to (U.S. Sen. Raphael Warnock) - The New Georgia Project... [i]t's among 35 cases involving potential violations of election law being sent from the State Election Board to the attorney general or local prosecutors...[t]he New Georgia Project, which bills itself as a nonpartisan effort to register voters, is accused of submitting 1,268 voter registration applications after the 10-day deadline to do so."[305]

Perhaps instances of voter fraud like this changed the outcome of the election - perhaps they did not. But in either case, the same problem remains; How do you prove beyond a reasonable doubt that Donald Trump did not believe his own assertions that he was cheated, and that he really won the 2020 Presidential election?

You can be sure that the former President will continue to make these assertions to anyone who will listen - which calls to mind another famous phrase by Yogi Berra - "It ain't over 'til it's over."

---

303 Ibid.
304 Ibid.
305 Anonymous, AP News, "Georgia: Potential vote fraud case handed to prosecutors", February 11, 2021

19 DIDN'T STACEY ABRAMS DENY LOSING HER ELECTION TOO?

Fulton County Georgia DA Fani Willis' 100-page indictment of former President Donald Trump, and 18 people involved in Trump's re-election campaign is all based on one, central allegation; "Defendant Donald John Trump lost the United States presidential election held on November 3, 2020. One of the states he lost was Georgia. Trump and the other Defendants charged in this Indictment refused to accept that Trump lost, and they knowingly and willfully joined [a] conspiracy to unlawfully change the outcome of the election in favor of Trump."[306]

All charges and allegations made in this indictment descend from this key assertion.

The same can be said for the federal indictment brought in Washington DC by Special Counsel Jack Smith. That document also states that "[t]he Defendant, DONALD J. TRUMP, was the forty-fifth President of the United States and a candidate for re-election in 2020. The Defendant lost the 2020 presidential election... [d]espite having lost...for more than two months following election day on November 3, 2020, the Defendant spread lies that there had been outcome-determinative fraud in the election and that he had actually won. These claims were false, and the Defendant knew that they were false. But the Defendant repeated and widely disseminated them anyway—to make his knowingly false claims appear legitimate, create an intense national atmosphere of mistrust and anger, and erode

[306] State of Georgia v. Donald J. Trump, et al., Indictment filed August 14, 2023, Fulton County Superior Court, Georgia

public faith in the administration of the election."[307]

We have discussed the difficulty in establishing that Trump knew he had actually lost (especially when so many of his fellow citizens also think Trump actually won), and in proving that the former President knew that his complaints of being cheated were false.

Yet, the unswerving position of the majority of the Democratic party and their supporters in the legal and legacy media establishments is that "election denial" is a crime in and of itself. For instance, according to the Brennan Center for Justice, Smith's "indictment amounts to another in a series of emphatic rejections of election denial since the 2020 election...[a] federal prosecutor has now weighed in, charging that the actions Trump took under the pretext of election denial were criminal...[o]ver the last two years, election denial has been proven false so many times that another debunking is unremarkable - this one, however, is historic in that it comes with charges against a former president."[308]

Then there is the Movement Advancement Project (MAP), "an independent nonprofit think tank that provides rigorous research, insight and communications that help speed equality and opportunity for all," which has issued a report entitled *How Election Denialism Threatens Our Democracy and the Safeguards We Need to Defend It.* The report "measures the level of risk to each state posed by election denialism, [and] the resulting threats when the proper safeguards are not in place...[t]he report includes MAP's new National Election Denial Risk Index, which shows that more than two in three American voters (157 million voters) live in states with at least a moderate risk of election denialism jeopardizing future elections. Of those, 29 million voters live in high-risk states for election denial." MAP asserts that their Index "is a tool for lawmakers, journalists, and the public that can be used to examine the range of ways that election denialism poses a threat to each state and which policies can strengthen a state's ability to combat these threats."[309]

One of MAP's recommended solutions to the "crime" of election

---

[307] United States of America v. Donald J. Trump, Indictment No. 23 CR 257, United States District Court, District of Columbia, August 1, 2023

[308] Ian Vanderwalker, Brennan Center for Justice, "Federal Indictment Is Another Rejection of Trump's Election Denial", August 1, 2023

[309] Movement Advancement Project, "How Election Denialism Threatens our Democracy and the Safeguards we Need to Defend it", May 2023

denial?

"[L]imiting partisan involvement in post-election processes, increasing penalties for election subversion, and limiting frivolous recount requests."[310]

Sure, who needs more free speech and participation in the democratic process? Certainly not the people at MAP!

And certainly not Jack Smith or Fani Willis.

But both seem to have their sights set on only one particular election denier and his followers. Aren't there other targets out there - others who denied they lost their election and refused to concede, creating the "threat" of "election denialism?"

As reported by *CNN*, "Democratic gubernatorial candidate Stacey Abrams defended herself from criticism that she never conceded her loss to Gov. Brian Kemp in 2018...Abrams, in the wake of her 2018 loss to Kemp by 1.4 percentage points, acknowledged that Kemp, who then worked as Georgia secretary of state, would be the governor of Georgia. But she specifically said in her final speech that she [would] not concede due to persistent voter suppression allegations, adding that conceding would mean acknowledging 'an action is right, true or proper' and 'as a woman of conscience and faith, I cannot concede that'...Abrams said Kemp 'won under the rules of the game at the time, but the game was rigged against the voters of Georgia...we had a system that [Kemp] managed, that he manipulated, hurt Georgia voters and the responsibility of leaders is to challenge systems that are not serving the people."[311]

Abrams also asserted that she has a "responsibility… to challenge a system that would rob a single voice from being able to be heard if they are eligible."[312] And just what did Abrams do to meet her "responsibility" to "challenge systems that are not serving the people?"

"A political organization backed by Democrat Stacey Abrams filed a federal lawsuit...challenging the way Georgia's elections are run, making good on a promise Abrams made as she ended her bid to become the state's governor...[the lawsuit] was filed by Fair Fight Action against interim Secretary of State Robyn Crittenden and state

---

310 Ibid.

311 Dan Merica, CNN, "Abrams defends lack of concession after 2018 gubernatorial loss", December 3, 2021

312 Ibid.

election board members in their official capacities...[a]s secretary of state, Abrams' opponent, Republican Gov.-elect Brian Kemp, was the top elections official until he declared himself the winner and resigned two days after the election...[t]he lawsuit was filed against Crittenden, who was appointed by Gov. Nathan Deal after Kemp stepped down, but it clearly targets Kemp."[313]

"Lauren Groh-Wargo, Abrams' campaign manager who's now CEO of Fair Fight Action [said] 'This lawsuit is going to look broadly at all the ways our secretary of suppression, Brian Kemp, suppressed the vote'... [o]n the campaign trail, Abrams repeatedly called Kemp 'an architect of suppression,' an allegation that Kemp vehemently denied."[314]

How did this effort to fight the "architect" of voter suppression in Georgia turn out?

"A federal judge [in 2022] found that Georgia election practices challenged by a group associated with Democrat Stacey Abrams do not violate the constitutional rights of voters, ruling in favor of the state on all remaining issues in a lawsuit filed nearly four years ago. 'Although Georgia's election system is not perfect, the challenged practices violate neither the constitution nor the VRA,' U.S. District Judge Steve Jones in Atlanta wrote, referring to the Voting Rights Act of 1965... Kemp...applauded the ruling...'Judge Jones' ruling exposes this legal effort for what it really is: a tool wielded by a politician hoping to wrongfully weaponize the legal system to further her own political goals,' Kemp said in a statement emailed by his campaign."[315]

In fact, "[w]hile Fair Fight collected stories from more than 3,000 voters, they found very few people who were unable to cast a ballot [in 2018] and none during the 2020 election...[i]nstead...the evidence showed that in many cases problems were resolved quickly once state officials were contacted."[316]

Further, Fair Fight Action "was ordered to repay $231,303.71 in

---

[313] Kate Brumback, PBS, "Lawsuit challenging Georgia election process filed by Stacey Abrams-backed group", November 27, 2018

[314] Ibid.

[315] Associated Press, NBC News, "Federal judge rules against Stacey Abrams group in voting rights lawsuit", September 30, 2022

[316] Digital Team, Fox5Atlanta, "Stacey Abrams group must pay back tax dollars for voter suppression lawsuit, judge orders", January 10, 2023

legal fees. $192,628.85 of that is for 'printed or electronically recorded transcripts necessarily obtained for use in the case.' The other $38,674.86 is for making copies to use in the case."[317]

In other words, in the 2018 Georgia Governor's race, Democrat Stacey Abrams refused to concede her loss to Republican Brian Kemp; she claimed Kemp was responsible for "voter suppression"; her campaign manager brought a lawsuit to challenge the results of the election; that lawsuit was ultimately unsuccessful; and despite Abrams' insistence, there was no "outcome determinative" fraud uncovered that would lead to the reversal of the election results.

How is this different from the actions Trump and his co-defendants are accused of taking to challenge the results of the 2020 Presidential election? According to Abrams, people should not conflate "her refusal to concede in the 2018 Georgia governor's race with former President Donald Trump's false claims of a stolen election, calling the latter wrong and dangerous for democracy. 'I will never ever say that it is OK to claim fraudulent outcomes as a way to give yourself power,' Abrams said...'[t]he issues that I raised in 2018 were not grounded in making me the governor...[n]ot a single lawsuit filed would have reversed or changed the outcome of the election. My point was that the access to the election was flawed, and I refuse to concede a system that permits citizens to be denied access. That is very different than someone claiming fraudulent outcome."[318]

Sure, now it makes sense. Abrams didn't think her assertions of voter suppression would change the result of the election she refused to concede - she just thought it was the right thing to do!

But this is exactly what she said in 2018: "Under the watch of the now former Secretary of State, democracy failed Georgians of every political party, every race, every region. Again. The incompetence and mismanagement we witnessed in this election had been on display months before...[b]ut this time, the mistakes clearly altered the outcome...I acknowledge that former Secretary of State Brian Kemp will be certified as the victor in the 2018 gubernatorial election. But to watch an elected official - who claims to represent the people of this state, baldly pin his hopes for election on the suppression of the people's democratic right to vote - has been truly appalling. So, to be

---

[317] Ibid

[318] Barbara Rodriguez, The 19th, "Stacey Abrams: It is 'wrong' to compare her refusal to concede with Trump's stolen election rhetoric", September 19, 2022

clear, this is not a speech of concession. Concession means to acknowledge an action is right, true or proper. As a woman of conscience and faith, I cannot concede." [319]

So, now it's clear - Trump asserted that the election was stolen from him, while Abrams claims her opponent suppressed votes, which caused her to lose. Trump filed a series of lawsuits that were mostly unsuccessful; Abrams' campaign filed one unsuccessful lawsuit.

But despite the lack of hard evidence to support Abrams' assertions, no one has claimed that Abrams was lying when she claimed that the suppression of the votes of those who supported her caused her to lose the election. In fact, as the court ruled in the lawsuit brought by Fair Fight Action, there was no evidence that voting was purposefully suppressed in Georgia - at all.

There are those who would argue that Abrams' assertion of voter suppression in 2018 was a lie. But others defend her statement as merely mistaken, and not intended to be untruthful. There are undoubtedly those who will tell you that Abrams was not lying, since she believed her own assertions of voter fraud.

But there seems to be only one real difference between the "lies" told by Donald Trump, and those told by Stacey Abrams. Trump's "lies" are being prosecuted by Fani Willis and Jack Smith. And Abrams' are not.

---

[319] Heather Timmons, Quartz, "Stacey Abrams' concession speech is a powerful critique of US civil rights", November 19, 2018

20 "A REALLY BIG BREAKTHROUGH FOR PROSECUTORS."

To date, the majority of our analysis of the RICO Indictment brought against Donald Trump and much of his 2020 election team has been centered on whether the allegations made are legally and facially sufficient. We have also examined some of the difficult issues that could face prosecutors who are required by law to establish their case "beyond a reasonable doubt." One such matter is the virtual impossibility of showing that Donald Trump did not truly believe that he won the 2020 Presidential election, and that voter suppression and fraud played a big part in his loss.

One tool that prosecutors use to meet their burden is to compel a co-defendant to testify against the "target" defendant. According to the Legal Information Institute of Cornell University, to "[t]urn state's evidence...or to "flip" means the defendant chose to reveal valuable evidence to the prosecutor, in exchange for a reduction of the charge or the dismissal of some charges. When the defendant 'flips' they are said to have 'turned state's evidence.' This is common in instances of organized crime when a defendant provides information on a co-defendant or other members' crimes. The defendant tries to flip for a better sentence..."[320]

In Georgia, several of the former President's co-defendants have entered guilty pleas to reduced charges, with the understanding that these defendants will cooperate, and probably testify, against Trump and the remaining co-defendants. One of those is lawyer Sidney

[320] Cornell Law School, Legal Information Institute, "turn state's evidence", undated

Powell.

As reported by *The Associated Press*, "Powell gained notoriety for threatening in a Fox Business interview in November 2020 to 'release the Kraken,' invoking a mythical sea monster when talking about a lawsuit she planned to file to challenge the results of the presidential election. Similar suits she filed in several states were promptly dismissed." Then, in October of 2023, "Powell...entered the plea just a day before jury selection was set to start in her trial. She pleaded guilty to six misdemeanors accusing her of conspiring to intentionally interfere with the performance of election duties. As part of the deal, she will serve six years of probation, will be fined $6,000 and will have to write an apology letter to Georgia and its residents. She also recorded a statement for prosecutors and agreed to testify truthfully against her co-defendants at future trials."[321]

The usual sources made the usual statements regarding Powell's plea. "This is a really big breakthrough for prosecutors," CNN senior legal analyst Elie Honig said...on *News Central.* "There's no such thing as halfway cooperation."[322]

What is Georgia DA Fani Willis expecting Powell to say in exchange for her plea deal? "The plea documents make clear that she's expected to testify about her direct involvement in the breach of election systems in Coffee County, Georgia, where a...group of Trump supporters (allegedly) collaborated with a local election official to access sensitive government data as part of their...search for massive voter fraud....Powell was also in touch with the Trump White House and other figures in Trump's orbit during the frenzied post-election period...Powell 'can [also] provide firsthand testimony about things [she] saw, things [she] overheard,' [according to] CNN legal analyst Elliot Williams."[323]

Soon after Powell entered her guilty plea, another of Donald Trump's co-defendants entered a guilty plea in Georgia. "Attorney and prominent conservative media figure Jenna Ellis pleaded guilty...to one felony count of aiding and abetting false statements and writings...She was sentenced to five years of probation along with $5,000 in restitution, 100 hours of community service, writing an

---

[321] Kate Brumback, AP News, "Sidney Powell pleads guilty over efforts to overturn Trump's loss in Georgia and agrees to cooperate", October 19, 2023

[322] Marshall Cohen, CNN, "How Sidney Powell's guilty plea may impact Donald Trump", October 20, 2023

[323] Ibid.

apology letter to the people of Georgia and testifying truthfully in trials related to this case."[324]

Once more, *CNN* expressed their belief that Trump was a "dead man walking." "These...plea deals are a monumental step forward for Fulton County District Attorney Fani Willis, who charged the case in August and is preparing for trials against Trump, his former attorney Rudy Giuliani, his chief of staff Mark Meadows and other top figures...Ellis...and Powell...agreed to testify on behalf of the prosecution at future trials. By flipping, these onetime Trump insiders are now on track to become major Trump nemeses. They...can shed light on what was happening behind the scenes in 2020."[325]

But in discussing Powell's anticipated cooperation, Williams made an interesting statement - "[i]f prosecutors aren't satisfied with the evidence that's provided, they can just yank this plea deal, and put these folks to trial."[326]

Not quite, Elliot.

While both Ellis and Powell have been sentenced, their cases are not legally concluded. A review of the third page of the plea agreement for Powell in particular states "[t]he Defendant consenting hereto, it is the judgment of the Court that no judgment of guilt be imposed at this time but that further proceedings are deferred...[u]pon fulfillment of the terms of this sentence, or upon release of the Defendant by the Court prior to the termination of this sentence, the Defendant shall stand discharged of said offense without court adjudication of guilt and shall be completely exonerated of guilt of said offense charged."[327]

This is known as a "conditional plea." Powell has obligated herself to testify in the trial of her co-defendants by her plea and has agreed to be truthful when she takes the stand (something that is expected of any witness, in any event). But the conditional nature of this plea agreement gives Powell a very powerful incentive to testify as Willis wants her to testify.

---

324 Will Weissert and Kate Brumback, AP News, "Jenna Ellis becomes latest Trump lawyer to plead guilty over efforts to overturn Georgia's election", October 24, 2003

325 Ibid.

326 Marshall Cohen, CNN, "How Sidney Powell's guilty plea may impact Donald Trump", October 20, 2023

327 State of Georgia v. Sidney Elizabeth Powell, Criminal Action No. 23SC190370, Final Disposition, Superior Court, Fulton County, Georgia, October 20, 2023

Inadvertently, in giving Powell this incentive, Willis may have handed Trump and his co-defendants a weapon they can use in their own defense.

In any trial, a jury (or the judge, if he or she is acting as factfinder without a jury) is charged with the responsibility to assess the credibility of any witness. "A credible witness is [one] who comes across as competent and worthy of belief. Their testimony is assumed to be more than likely true due to their experience, knowledge, training, and sense of honesty...[a]n attorney can show jurors a witness is not credible by showing: 1) inconsistent statements, 2) reputation for untruthfulness, 3) defects in perception, 4) prior convictions that show dishonesty or untruthfulness, and 5) bias."[328] "Bias" is defined as "to exhibit a pre-existing inclination or prejudice for or against someone or something. In the context of evidence in criminal law, bias is used to describe the relationship between a party and a witness which might lead the witness to unconsciously or otherwise, give testimony in favor of or against a party."[329]

Clearly, whether or not the witness has "turned state's evidence" and is awaiting a favorable adjudication of their own charges in exchange for their testimony is an obvious source of bias.

For instance, in the 1984 Rhode Island case of *State v. Beaumier*, in "a robbery trial...the state's primary witness was a Providence Police officer and friend of the defendant. According to this officer, defendant admitted to him his participation in the robbery. Defense counsel attempted to cross-examine the officer as to thefts at a lumberyard in which the officer was a suspect and under investigation. Counsel was attempting to show that the officer had a motive to fabricate defendant's admission in order to ingratiate himself with his superiors. The trial judge precluded this area of inquiry."[330]

In reversing the conviction, the Rhode Island appellate court stated that "[t]he right of confrontation is concerned with the proposition that a jury be allowed to evaluate any motive that a witness may have for testifying. That right is especially precious where, as here, the motive may belong to the state's prime witness. It

[328] Cornell Law School, Legal Information Institute, "credible witness", undated

[329] Cornell Law School, Legal Information Institute, "bias", undated

[330] John MacDonald, Rhode Island Criminal Defense Practice Manual, 4th Edition, "Cross Examination Bias, Motive and Prejudice", 2011

is clear, therefore, that the evidence concerning the investigation should have been admitted...in the final analysis, it is the jury that should consider the evidence and reach its own conclusion."[331]

Spencer Martinez, writing for the *Cleveland State Law Review*, notes that "[i]n spite of advances in scientific and statistical evidence, the success of a criminal prosecution continues to hinge primarily on witness testimony. Such evidence is difficult to come by, especially in the case of more sophisticated criminals or defendants who commit crimes through syndicates that insulate them from the relevant actus reus. Therefore, prosecutors must often look to other criminals for case-building testimony. Eliciting testimony from such witnesses often requires that a 'deal' be struck, whereby the government promises the guilty witness some degree of leniency for his cooperation. 'Bargaining' for witness testimony in this fashion has long been recognized as a legitimate, necessary practice. However, the ramifications of such agreements have always caused concern for those involved with defendants' rights, as the cooperating witness has a strong incentive to commit perjury to reap the full benefit of the 'contract.' This is especially true now that agreements are becoming more liberal with respect to what the government may offer the cooperating witness, what the witness is obligated to do in return, and how the witness is to suffer in the event he fails to perform or fails to secure the desired effect. Clearly the most important safeguard against false testimony is the defendant's right to cross-examine the cooperating witness as to bias. The defendant's discretion to probe into cooperation agreements, however, is not on par with the government's increasing discretion in what it may offer a criminal witness in exchange for his testimony."[332]

A Georgia jury is free to believe Powell and Ellis. But they are also free to believe that each has a strong incentive to testify as DA Willis wishes them to testify.

Thus, having these co-defendants testify against Trump and the other defendants is not a positive development for the defense. But is it the "really big breakthrough" *CNN* commentators hope it to be?

Probably not.

---

[331] State v. Beaumier, 480 A2d 1367 (Rhode Island, 1984)

[332] Spencer Martinez, Bargaining for Testimony: Bias of Witnesses Who Testify in Exchange for Leniency , 47 Cleveland State Law Review 141 (1999)

IN CONCLUSION - THE MAKING OF A MARTYR

According to the Merrian-Webster dictionary, a Martyr is "a person who voluntarily suffers death as the penalty of witnessing to and refusing to renounce a religion." This description does not, in any way, fit the current situation faced by former President Donald Trump. However, there is a secondary definition that describes the plight of the 45th President very closely; "a person who sacrifices something of great value and especially life itself for the sake of principle."

According to the *BBC*, "Donald Trump's net worth dropped by about $700m to $2.3bn... during his time as president." Citing to a study conducted by the Bloomberg Billionaires Index, "Bloomberg analysed financial documents and other filings from May 2016 and January 2021 to calculate Mr Trump's wealth before and after he became US president." Some of this loss was attributed to the Covid-19 pandemic, and the reduction in value and revenue in his real estate and golf club holdings as a result of the extensive lockdowns. But other reasons for former President Trump's losses are also described; "After the Capitol Hill siege in January, the Professional Golfers' Association (PGA) of America ended an agreement to host its 2022 championship tournament at Mr Trump's New Jersey golf course, saying it would hurt the group's brand. Deutsche Bank, the only bank willing to lend to him after his bankruptcies in the 1990s, also said after the riots that it would not do business with him again."[333]

---

[333] Justin Harper, BBC, "Donald Trump's wealth takes tumble during presidency", March 17, 2021

Besides losing these business relationships after the January 6 riots, Trump was also famously excluded from social media. "Remember when Donald Trump was permanently banned from Twitter and 'indefinitely' suspended from Facebook following the attack of the Capitol on January 6?" asks *Glamour* Magazine. "On January 8, Discord, an instant messaging and chatroom app popular with teens, banned a server called TheDonald.win...'[w]hile there is no evidence of the server being used to organize the Jan 6 riots, Discord decided to ban the entire server...due to its overt connection to an online forum used to incite violence and plan an armed insurrection in the United States,' a Discord rep said in a statement...Instagram, which is owned by Facebook, also banned Trump from posting, per head of Instagram Adam Mosseri."[334]

The New York Times noted that "[w]hen Facebook and Twitter barred Donald J. Trump from their platforms after the Capitol riot in January, he lost direct access to his most powerful megaphones...[b]efore the ban, the social media post with the median engagement generated 272,000 likes and shares. After the ban, that dropped to 36,000 likes and shares."[335]

Instead of calling for these social media companies to reverse their bans, the *BBC* suggested that "the most obvious way Mr Trump can profit post-presidency is with a news channel or social media platform that would appeal to his 74m voters in the 2020 election."[336]

In fact, Trump did create his own social media platform - *Truth Social.* But has that worked out for him financially? Not according to *CBS News*; "[a] new regulatory filing reveals that Truth Social's owner, Trump Media & Technology Group, has booked only $2.3 million in sales through June this year, while losing 10 times that amount...[t]he financial details about Trump Media & Technology Group were made public in a...filing from Digital World Acquisition Corp. (DWAC), a so-called special-purpose acquisition company, or SPAC, formed to merge with Trump's business...[t]he financial picture that emerges from [the] filing depicts a company that's facing

334 Emily Tannenbaum, Glamour, "Every Social Media Platform Donald Trump Is Banned From Using (So Far)", June 4, 2021

335 Davy Alba, Ella Koeze, and Jacob Silver, The New York Times, "What Happened When Trump Was Banned on Social Media", June 7, 2021

336 Justin Harper, BBC, "Donald Trump's wealth takes tumble during presidency", March 17, 2021

mounting losses in the face of growing, yet meager, sales. Trump Media reported revenue of $2.3 million for the first six months of 2023, compared with no revenue in the year-earlier period, the filing noted. With its losses mounting, Trump Media is also burning through cash, ending June with $2.4 million in cash, down from $19 million a year earlier, according to [the] filing. The company reported an operating loss of $23.3 million in 2022, although it recorded a $50.5 million net profit after a change in value tied to its convertible notes."[337]

Obviously, removing Trump from social media platforms like Facebook and Twitter were intended to financially hurt him. Equally obvious is that those efforts have been successful - and even more obvious, is the absolute glee taken by some in these efforts to silence Donald Trump. "Trump's lies and rhetoric found an eager audience online – one that won't disappear when his administration ends. Experts warn the platforms will continue to be used to organize and perpetuate violence," according to *The Guardian.* "Trump's leverage of social media to spread propaganda has gone largely unchecked'...said Jennifer M Grygiel, assistant professor of communication at Syracuse University and expert on social media...'What happened (January 6) is the product of four years of systematic propaganda from the presidency,' Grygiel said."[338]

When considering the financial harm done to Trump, his legal fees must be added to the list. "Trump's Save America political action committee has paid nearly $37 million to more than 60 law firms and individual attorneys since January 2022, Federal Election Commission records show. That amounts to more than half of the PAC's total expenditures, according to an Associated Press analysis of campaign finance filings, and represents a staggering sum compared to other political organizations."[339] Further, "legal experts consulted by Reuters said Trump's defense in four criminal prosecutions could cost over $50 million, more than all the money

[337] Aimee Picchi, CBS News, "Donald Trump's Truth Social has lost $23 million this year. Its accountants warn it may not survive", November 14, 2023
[338] Karl Paul, The Guardian, "'Four years of propaganda': Trump social media bans come too late, experts say", January 8, 2021
[339] Richard Lardner, Trenton Daniel, and Aaron Kessler, AP News, "Lawyers, Trump and money: Ex-president spends millions in donor cash on attorneys as legal woes grow", October 17, 2023

raised in the first half of this year by Trump's campaign and its top allied super PAC, Make America Great Again Inc, known as MAGA Inc."[340]

As reported in *The Hill*, "[i]n a speech to supporters in Sioux City, Iowa, Trump claimed he lost billions of dollars going into politics and lamented the cost of his legal fees. 'It's cost me a couple of billion dollars to be a politician. Everyone else makes, they make [money]. I said, 'No, we can't do that.' I could have made a fortune. The countries are coming [and saying,] 'We'd like to build a job and we'd like to have you involved.' Billions. I say, I tell my kids, 'Sorry, kids, we can't do it. I'm president.' I respected the office,' Trump said."[341]

Reviewing these facts is not an effort to elicit your sympathies for former President Trump. However, this litany of lost opportunities, out of pocket expenses and financial reversals does justify the description of the 45th President as a Martyr - someone who "sacrifices something of great value...for the sake of principle."

The description of a Martyr includes someone who sacrifices their life. This account could also fit the 77-year-old 45th President, for as *Forbes* notes, "Trump has been indicted on 91 federal and state charges in total [and is] facing a range of felony charges that all carry potential prison sentences that add up to a potential maximum sentence of 717.5 years in prison."[342]

Why did he do it? Why did Trump run for President of the United States in 2016, and then fight so hard for the Office after the results of the 2020 election were announced?

For one thing, Donald Trump is notoriously stubborn. "Trump's temper has been a constant force in [his] White House," according to *Politico*. "For Trump, anger serves as a way to manage staff, express his displeasure or simply as an outlet that soothes him. Often, aides and advisers say, he'll get mad at a specific staffer or broader situation, unload from the Oval Office and then three hours later act as if nothing ever occurred even if others still feel rattled by it.

[340] Jason Lange et al., Reuters, "Trump's campaign machine is bleeding cash for legal expenses", September 29, 2023

[341] Sarah Fortinsky, The Hill, "Trump says he has $100M in legal fees amid cascade of court battles", October 29, 2023

[342] Alison Durkee, Forbes, "Trump's Total Charges Could Result In More Than 700 Years In Prison—Here's Why That's So Unlikely", Augugst 16, 2023

Negative television coverage and lawyers earn particular ire from him. White House officials and informal advisers say the triggers for his temper are if he thinks someone is lying to him, if he's caught by surprise, if someone criticizes him, or if someone stops him from trying to do something or seeks to control him."[343]

According to *MSNBC* commentator Al Sharpton, "[a]s a native New Yorker, I have watched Donald Trump's star rise and fall over the past 30 years...[n]o matter the scenario, Trump was always a consummate narcissist and self-promoter. But these qualities were not the most disturbing things about him - many politicians and businessmen act in similar ways. What disturbed me the most was that he never ever showed a different side of himself...he was not driven by ideology or a sense of a broader purpose. He did whatever he could to enrich his coffers and build his brand. This was his main motivation in 1989, and it remains his main motivation in 2017."[344]

Of course, we must take Sharpton's assessment with the proverbial grain of salt. As described by *The New York Times*, "sometimes they were friends in the way that public figures in New York can be. Mr. Trump cut the ribbon at Mr. Sharpton's National Action Network annual convention in 2002, returning four years later to pose with Mr. Sharpton, the Rev. Jesse Jackson and the singer James Brown...the two were...'classic New York characters,' recalled George Arzt, the press secretary to Mayor Edward I. Koch. 'There was a clash of who is the loudest voice in New York,' he said, adding that the two made Mr. Koch's tenure...more difficult. 'Koch's problem as mayor is that he had Trump on one side and Al Sharpton on the other side,' Mr. Arzt said."[345]

In other words, it takes one shameless self-promoter to believe he knows another.

It is also a gross oversimplification of Donald Trump's motives to blame his "stubbornness" and "drive for self-promotion" on his unwavering contention that he won the 2020 Presidential election, and that the Office of the President was stolen from him. If Trump's

---

[343] Nancy Cook and Josh Dawsey, Politico, '"He is stubborn and doesn't realize how bad this is getting"', August 16, 2017

[344]The Reverand Al Sharpton, NBC News, "President Trump Is Exactly the Same Selfish Blowhard I Knew Back In New York", November 8, 2017

[345] James Barron and Jeffrey C Mays, The New York Times, "How Trump and Sharpton Became the Ultimate New York Frenemies", July 29, 2019

intention was to "build his brand" with his Presidency, his losses certainly prove that effort unsuccessful.

Instead, the fault does not lie with Donald Trump. The objective facts show that the former President did not "lead an insurrection" on January 6, 2021; mostly because there is scant evidence that an actual "insurrection," as opposed to a riot, occurred at the Capitol that day. In this regard, Trump's words at the Ellipse that day cannot, in any reasonable estimation, be viewed as "incitement to insurrection." In fact, his words do not support an accusation of "incitement to riot" either.

The facts, as we have reviewed them in the preceding chapters, also show that Donald Trump sincerely believed he had won the 2020 Presidential election; that there was a basis to believe that voter fraud had occurred in a variety of states; and that he believed his efforts to either delay or overturn the results of that election were legal and legitimate.

Further, the facts clearly and unequivocally show that the search of Mar A Lago was illegal, based upon an overbroad search warrant that did not conform to the standards required by the Fourth Amendment; that Trump had a legal basis for the retention of the classified documents found during that illegal search; and that Special Counsel Jack Smith has used a variety of ethically and legally questionable tactics in his efforts to prosecute former President Trump.

What the facts also show, is that Donald Trump is being criminally charged with offenses that could apply equally to his opponent in the 2016 Presidential election. The New York State indictment, much of which is beyond the Statute of Limitations, accuses Trump of falsifying his campaign records to disguise a payment to porno actress Stormy Daniels. As we discussed in our Introduction, the Hillary Clinton campaign admitted to classifying their costs in assembling the Steele Dossier as a campaign expense, a violation of Campaign Finance laws, and paid a fine to the Federal Election Commission. Yet, despite former Senator Clinton's ties to New York (including her residence in that state), Manhattan DA Alvin Bragg has not sought to indict the former First Lady for falsifying her business records.

Similarly, Jack Smith's first federal indictment of Donald Trump relates to the classified documents seized during the illegal search of Mar A Lago. Yet, current President Joe Biden also maintained classified documents at his residence, most dating to his Vice-Presidency, when he had no ability to declassify those documents. To date, the investigation of President Biden continues, while the Indictment of the 45th President was brought in record time.

It is also worthy of note that both Smith and Georgia DA Fani Willis have based some of their allegations on Donald Trump's failure to concede the 2020 Presidential Election, while no such prosecution exists against Stacey Abrams for her failure to concede her loss in 2018 of the Georgia gubernatorial election.

We have not emphasized this blatant two-tiered system of justice here in these pages; instead, we have tried to review each indictment on its own merits (and lack thereof) as a Court would do.

Simply put, it is not a defense to any criminal charge that you're being prosecuted while someone else who did the same thing is walking around free. A defendant must answer to the charges brought against him or her, and a Court is duty bound to consider only whether the state can prove that defendant guilty of those charges.

There is no room for "whataboutism" in a courtroom - so there hasn't been much room for it here. But this isn't a courtroom, so some attention has been paid to this topic, while understanding Trump's defense in each case cannot rely on this issue.

It is also crucial to note a factor that weighs heavily in Donald Trump's favor. Due to the "Swamp's" naked hatred and fear of the former President, these professional bureaucrats and the political officeholders they support have lost sight of something fundamental. In general, Americans do not like bullies, and don't like to see someone being bullied.

Sure, many Trump-haters believe the 45th President to be a bully himself. But more Americans see Trump being bullied by lawyers bringing prosecutions which do not withstand legal scrutiny. According to *Reuters*, "[s]small donors have responded to Donald Trump's legal problems by showering money on his presidential campaign...[m]ore than $2 million surged into Trump's coffers within a day of the Aug. 24 release of his mugshot after he was booked at a jail on Georgia state charges...according to a disclosure the campaign submitted to the Federal Election Commission."[346]

---

[346] Jason Lange and Alexander Ulmer, Reuters, "Trump's legal troubles keep fueling surges in fundraising", October 16, 2023

And then there is that mugshot. Writing for *The Guardian*, columnist Arwa Mahdawi seems dumbfounded by the power of the Donald; "While any normal person would find it mortifying to have become the first former president to face 91 charges in four criminal cases and have a booking photo taken, Trump is busy slapping his mugshot on merchandise and inserting it into fundraising efforts. Trump is seizing control of the narrative as much as he possibly can, and attempting to turn his mugshot into a badge of honour rather than disgrace."[347]

Attempting? As we noted above, people have responded to the release of that infamous mugshot - just not in the way Mahdawi and other Trump detractors had hoped. "Donald Trump has turned his Georgia mugshot into a record-breaking fundraising haul," Politico states. "The former president has raised $7.1 million since he was booked at an Atlanta jail Thursday evening (August 24, 2023), according to figures provided...by his campaign. On Friday (August 25, 2023) alone, Trump raised $4.18 million, making it the single-highest 24-hour period of his campaign to date, according to a person familiar with the totals."[348]

Why did so many people help Donald Trump turn his disgrace into a triumph? As we said - because many people view the former President as being bullied and fighting back against those bullies. Even before Trump's New York County Indictment, Republican Governor of New Hampshire, Chris Sununu said "I think it's building a lot of sympathy for the former president...I just think that not just the media, but really, a lot of the Democrats have misplayed this in terms of building sympathy for the former president, and it does drastically change the paradigm as we go into the 2024 election."[349]

Writing in *Politico*, former federal prosecutor Ankush Khardori agrees; "Sometimes even Donald Trump has a point. This time, it's his claim that he has been singled out...for conduct that would probably not have been charged as a crime against anyone else...[t]he

347 Arwa Mahdawi, The Guardian, "Trump is turning his mugshot into a badge of honour – but will voters see it that way?", August 26, 2023
348 Alex Isenstadt, Politico, "Trump raised $7.1 million after Georgia booking, mugshot", August 26, 2023
349 Aubrie Spady, Fox News, "Rumored 2024 contender says Dems are rallying support for Trump's campaign, 'misplayed' possible indictment", March 20, 2023

claim is likely to be a central part of Trump's defense, both in the public and legal arenas, and it is not likely to go away anytime soon - particularly since there is good reason to believe that it's true."[350]

In discussing the Bragg indictment, Khardon continues; "We are likely to hear a lot of clichés from the legal commentariat in the coming days — about how Bragg and his prosecutors are simply following the facts and the law, about how no one is above the law, and so on. That is all well and good, but the reality is that this particular criminal case probably never would have been brought for anyone but Trump. In fact, the investigation probably would not have begun in the first place for anyone else...the Manhattan DA's office was a convenient outlet and prosecutorial avenue for people who wanted to see Trump criminally prosecuted."[351]

Though Khardon is no supporter of the former President, he has hit upon the underlying truth of these prosecutions - that no one but Donald Trump would be charged with these crimes. Not Hillary Clinton. Not Joe Biden. Only Donald Trump.

This underlying truth is the basis for the feeling that Trump is being bullied, and the more he resists his bullies, the more support he gains.

It bears repeating - Americans do not like bullies. Especially when they are government employees, US Senators and Congress members, newscasters, commentators, and journalists - and most especially when the allegations made against the former President are so transparently insufficient and largely unsustainable as criminal acts.

So even if Donald Trump cannot use this "whataboutism" in his defense at any of his trials, the perception of the "Swamp" singling out and bullying the former President explains his strong public support to date in the run up to the 2024 Presidential Election.

Of course, it doesn't help that the perception is correct - political opponents of Donald Trump are misusing their authority to bring a series of legally questionable charges against the former President - and in doing so, the Swamp is making a political Martyr of Donald J. Trump.

---

[350] Ankush Khardori, Politico, "Opinion | Trump Seems to Be the Victim of a Witch Hunt. So What?", March 30, 2023

[351] Ibid.

ABOUT THE AUTHOR

For more than 30 years, John H. Wilson participated in all phases of the litigation process, from being counsel for both the plaintiff and defense in personal injury matters, to the prosecution and defense of criminal matters, to being the court itself.

Judge Wilson served as an Assistant District Attorney in Bronx County, New York. He was a trial attorney for the in-house counsel for a major insurance carrier and has also managed both a private practice and a boutique law firm, handling both plaintiff's personal injury and criminal defense matters. He was elected to the Civil Court, Bronx County in 2004, and served as a Judge in the Criminal Courts of New York City for ten years, presiding primarily in Brooklyn and the Bronx.

After his retirement from the NYC bench, he served as the Chief Prosecutor for the Standing Rock Reservation in Fort Yates, North Dakota, and then as a Mediator for First Court in Mandan, North Dakota.

Judge Wilson has published in various Law Reviews, written a series of articles for the *New York Law Journal*, and has published numerous case decisions. He is the author of a children's book, *Hot House Flowers*, available on Amazon.com.

He writes frequently for usagovpolicy.com and for his own Substack blog, *The Daily Outrage*. (https://johnhwilson.substack.com/). He is also a frequent guest on the *Vernuccio/Novak Report*, which is available on Rumble: (https://rumble.com/user/AmericanAnalysisofNewsandMedia).

Currently, Judge Wilson is retired from the practice of law, and resides in the Free State of Florida.

Made in the USA
Middletown, DE
03 January 2025